If You Don't Laugh You'll Cry

T0385406

ANGIE KENT

If You Don't Laugh You'll Cry

hachette
AUSTRALIA

Published in Australia and New Zealand in 2019
by Hachette Australia
(an imprint of Hachette Australia Pty Limited)
Level 17, 207 Kent Street, Sydney NSW 2000
www.hachette.com.au

10 9 8 7 6 5 4 3 2 1

 A catalogue record for this
book is available from the
National Library of Australia

ISBN: 978 0 7336 4329 3

Cover design by Christabella Designs
Cover photography and studio shots by Rob Palmer
All other photographs from the collection of Angie Kent
Typeset in Sabon LT Std by Kirby Jones
Printed and bound in Great Britain by Clays Ltd, Elcograf S.p.A.

 The paper this book is printed on is certified against the Forest Stewardship Council® Standards. McPherson's Printing Group holds FSC® chain of custody certification SA-COC-005379. FSC® promotes environmentally responsible, socially beneficial and economically viable management of the world's forests.

This book is dedicated to all the people in my life I have learnt from and who have loved me no matter what.

But mostly, this book is dedicated to my Nanny Fae Bindon. May your legacy of love, light, purity and faith in everything that surrounded you live on. I love you, my blue butterfly. Be free.

Contents

Dear diary ...

Ha! Totally kidding! I'm not that lame. Well, I kinda am ... but I won't do that to you all. Not this soon into our reading experience.

Firstly, I would like to start off by saying I am not a writer. These are just my own personal thoughts, opinions and experiences blurted out in text form as best as I possibly can with my bad Queensland education (just joking, in case any of my old teachers happen to read this).

If you don't like/agree with what I have to write, well, don't look, darling – just don't look!

Again, I'm only kidding. But, seriously, you don't have to agree at all. We couldn't all possibly agree on everything. How incredibly boring would life be if we all agreed?

I have slowly but surely been drowning in the excessive amount of creative juices that have built up over time due to lack of use. So what better way to release these juices than to annoy those of you who actually want to read the dross that fills my mind? (I promise as time goes on my grammar and spelling will get better and the content will become much better too.)

I don't even think that last sentence was very good English (and neither was that).

Truly, though, everyone has a story. Share and inspire people with yours. You have a story to tell so own it.

I feel deeply about everything I have been through and experienced so I am owning it and sharing it with you. Who am I to inspire anyone? I am no one but myself and my story. And my story could inspire others. Just as yours can too.

Most of all, I want this book to be about sharing. Sharing with those of you brave enough to read the words of a mad woman. I want to share with you my thoughts, my experience with mindfulness, meditation, spirituality, relationships, friendships and mental health, and mainly just to have a good ol' laugh. The good people of the planet were not joking when they said laughter is the best medicine. I preach that like nobody's business. I ask that you be open minded. Take what you will and enjoy the ride. Here we go ...

CHAPTER 1

Here and Now

Let's start off with a little back tale about the last few years and why I think they've had such a huge impact on where and who I am at this very moment.

The last few years have been incredibly unusual, to say the least. I cannot speak for everyone, but it certainly has been a bloody stirring few years for me and for quite a lot of people I know.

If you love all things universe and planet-to-mood-related you will also be a huge believer in the Saturn Return.

But some of you might ask, 'What is the Saturn Return?'

With the first Saturn Return of their life, a person will leave their youth and enter adulthood. It takes about 29.5 years for the Saturn Return to meet your natal Saturn – basically, where the planet Saturn was when you were born. The Saturn Return generally hits in the late twenties and continues into your early thirties.

Long story short, Saturn Return can be a right ball-ache and when it is done you finally find your place in this weird and wacky world. Please take the time if you have not already to Google Saturn Return if you are just reaching what I have felt to be the most hectic time of my life (mid to late twenties). I highly recommend you prepare yourself and know that you are in for quite the ride.

I can tell you this much, I have never been so happy to be twenty-nine. Twenty-nine has been my year, ladies and gents! Watch this space! There's more to come from thirty.

Lately I've had many realisations and I have found that I am **almost** a completely different person in the way I think and feel about nearly everything. (**Almost** is in **bold** because I still have a lot of old-school tendencies that surely need some work, and some that I love and don't really want to ship out. They can stick around.)

I grew up in a coasty environment, and unless you moved away there was a solid chance your destiny was marriage and kidlets at quite a young age. Perhaps own a nice little dress store or cafe or something along those lines. NOT that there is anything wrong with that at all. That was just never for me.

I always said that all I wanted was to get out of the Sunshine Coast and to become a successful director and/or producer, travel and just live my damn life however I want to live it. Despite society's expectations.

Originally I was mad about theatre (don't know why, I guess I just LOVED to perform) then that turned into wanting to make it within the film and/or television production industry. Mainly documentaries. I was mad for them.

When I first moved to Sydney back in December 2011, after studying Creative Industries at QUT in Brisbane, all I wanted was to work my butt off and be well respected for being a ridiculously hard worker. Not some 21-year-old who would just twirl her hair and hope for the best.

I prided myself on being a strong, independent woman 'who don't need no man'! I still to this day have that thought in the back of my mind. I've managed to embed this whole I-am-a-solo-woman-hear-me-roar in my mind pretty hardcore. I felt like I could not have both this really great career and a boyfriend (and, yes, I realise what that sounds like in light of something significant I'm undertaking this year, but we'll get to that later).

So I well and truly managed to push away a good man at the time and pretty much have never had one since.

I think the reason behind this was because I had only really seen the women in my life have one or the other.

They could have a family but no solid career ambitions, or vice versa.

While I was growing up my parents played their gender-specific roles to a T. My mum was very much there to raise us kids and cook and clean, and my dad worked hard and made most of the family-based decisions. My mum and dad didn't have much of a romantic relationship, from what I saw.

I had a very strong aunty who I saw go off and travel the world and be a gypsy and date lots of different guys, and I thought, *Yes! This is more of what I want. I want to travel the world, and date all the right people at the wrong time.* (Or all the wrong people at the right time – depends on which way you want to look at it, really.)

I knew from a young age that I only wanted a relationship where I was equal with my partner. We would have our roles in our careers but when we came home the only role we had was loving each other and bringing out the best in each other.

I had not actually seen this type of relationship, therefore I avoided finding out if it was really possible. I feel that is where this whole I-can't-have-both idea came from.

As I have grown up I've realised that this is not the case: the right person will love and support you and never expect you to play a role just because society used to make us believe that this was the way things should be. Men can cry and stay at home and look after the kids if that is what both of you want. Women can get down and dirty and fix cars or whatever the hell they want to fix.

Gender roles are stupid. That's my feeling towards that subject. Now let's move on, shall we?

Back to talking about when I moved to Sydney: I would work fifteen-hour days; I was ridiculously underweight and hardly slept due to being so anxious about trying to be perfect at everything I did. This happened especially at work.

I wanted to look like I could work as hard as any man in that office, and boy oh boy did I ever. When it came to having a day off, I would binge-drink and go out and paint the town red.

Ultimately, by the end of the night, I would manage to start a 'poor me' fight with a lot of nearest and dearest, because my subconscious was wanting me to vent one way or another. I was exhausted after trying to be so damn perfect, kind, giving, always there to solve everyone's problems day in and day out.

There is lesson number one, dear friends: numbing your pain with booze is not the answer!!!

I feel there is this cultural agreement that us Australians have made somewhere along the line where if you don't drink until you're absolutely wasted then you are just not doing it right. It is so culturally acceptable to binge-drink here and it is so wrong.

But that was all I knew. I was born and bred watching my parents drink too much. Alcoholism is huge on the Kent side of the family. And frighteningly life ruining. The Kent men would work hard and drink even harder. I believe drinking is what killed my dear Poppy Ted. He most probably would not have had three strokes that eventually turned him into a vegetable for the last part of his life if he hadn't spent years binge-drinking copious amounts of alcohol day and night. This is just my opinion, of course. I am obviously no doctor and I guess we will never know the real answer, but from what I have seen and experienced I know in my mind and heart that drinking that much has never done anyone any good.

All I do now is hope and pray that my father will cut down on his booze. Maybe after reading this he will. Maybe not. I know I love my family with all my heart and all my soul and only want what is best for them, and I know that drinking as much as some of them do is not the answer to the happiness they deserve.

You don't drink your body weight in booze if you are happy. I know this because I have done it at times in my life and most of those times were not when I was loving life. They were when I was at my lowest.

Social drinking is fabulous. I love a cheeky boozy night when celebrating or attending an event. Anything more than that I know that I am pushing the limits. Especially nowadays. This old grey mare, she ain't what she used to be.

BUT WAIT – there is a silver lining: I have learnt from my mistakes – yay!

Well, I am *learning* …

As I get older I realise how important happiness is. I always thought my happiness was to be a woman who could do everything herself and didn't need no man. If I didn't have a man or didn't rely on anyone else, then no one could take away my happiness. I just didn't think my little heart could handle that kind of loss. I wanted so badly to have a fancy-shmancy title at a well-respected production company and show everyone that you don't need to get married and be someone's wife to be … 'someone'. I have just seen so many relationships not be equal. Especially with my mother and father, and my grandparents.

Growing up I also experienced such an interesting relationship with my father that after all that hurt I could not imagine allowing someone who hadn't born me to treat me so terribly. I thought if my own dad could sometimes pretend I didn't even exist, then what could someone who was not my dad do to me?

I don't like to touch on this too much as I don't want my dad to think I don't love him more than anything and that I don't appreciate everything he has done for me and my family. I do believe that because of his upbringing he has suffered in ways that you couldn't even imagine, hence the way he was towards us kids from time to time. I also respect that this story is not my story to tell: it is his story.

Rest assured that we now have the best relationship that we have had since I was the apple of his eye when I was first born and his little girl. I guess that one day I will sit down and ask him why he did certain things and behaved in certain ways – but I know one thing for sure, and that is that I would never question his love for me and I hope he never questions my love for him. Without some of his MOP ways (Mental Old Prick is his nickname when he is acting out) I would not be the person I am today. I was raised by one of the most generous men and one of the funniest bastards you could ever meet.

I also believe this 'I can do it ma'self, asshole' attitude came from having seen so many women invest all their happiness into one person and then when that person took it all away from them they literally felt they had nothing.

So, because of this very strong yet very misguided way of thinking, I have almost made myself despise relationships – and that hasn't made me happy at all. Where is the happiness in that?

This extreme way of thinking has obviously not come from nowhere; it of course stems from having seen interesting relationships growing up and experiencing some myself.

Them damn daddy issues – you could smell that coming, I'm sure. I feel many of us here in Australia seem to have them.

CHAPTER 2

Childhood

My childhood was what I believe to be your everyday stock-standard Aussie childhood but with a few little hurdles and quirks along the way.

I was the first born. Came out looking like a cone head 'cause my poor little noggin got stuck and it was flattened like a pancake. It stayed like that for a few days.

I believe this is why I have a ginormous forehead and got a nickname from my very own father, Forehead Fred. Cheers, Dad, you sure know how to make a gal feel special.

I don't mind the big ol' forehead now. I feel the bigger the forehead the bigger the brain, really.

Apparently I was a very difficult baby and cried day and night. Mum did find out that I was a colicky baby – this meant I could cry inconsolably for several hours at a time.

Lucky Mum. Her first little bundle of joy was a screaming asshole with a massive flattened head. Cute.

I remember being very loved. Though Mum told me later down the track that we went to live with her parents for a couple of months after I was born because I was so difficult and Mum and Dad were not getting on. To be fair, they'd only really met a year before I arrived and Dad whisked Mum overseas for a pretty solid world trip and got her pregnant in Paris.

They were going to call me Paris. Thank god they didn't as I was in my peak teenage years when Paris Hilton's porn tape came out. Could you imagine the bulk banter I would have copped surrounding that?

I already got the delightfully catchy nickname Phalange – because 'Angie Phalange' almost rhymes, doesn't it, and the boys at school just thought they were such clever clogs. It stuck pretty much my entire high school life, so I guess they were quite clever after all.

Dad won Mum back after a solid amount of time apart and they got married when I was eighteen months old. I think it's pretty bohemian that I got to attend my mum and dad's wedding. Running around the old-school 90s-themed church with all the 90s-themed attire with a bottle full of juice to shut me the hell up. The 90s, when you could fill your toddler's bottle with pure sugar and no one would judge you. Nowadays, could you imagine the absolute disgust in every modern mother's eyes? Christ on a bendy bicycle, the thought alone gives me anxiety.

Mum, Dad and I moved around a lot in my baby years and when I was three along came Bradley Mark Kent. For the next two years it was just us. The two best friends that anyone could have. I would say 'Jump' and Brad would say 'How high, Ashgie?' (That is how Brad would pronounce my name.)

When I look at family home videos now, I love listening to our little accents and our own little language. It is just so incredibly old-school Aussie that I crack up when I hear it.

Then along came Joshua Edward Kent.

I could probably do an essay alone on what Josh and my family went through when he arrived. Josh was born with a partial closure of the valve on his bladder, causing his kidneys to blow up, which then led to constant infections. Josh had an operation called a ureterostomy, which brought his ureter to the skin to rest his kidneys. So growing up we thought it was normal to see our baby brother do his wee through a bag for eighteen months. We called it his built-in peenie.

Dad and my mumma, Jane, a.k.a. Ma Sweet, were in and out of hospital with Josh for weeks on end. Josh had seven operations by the time he was six years old. My sweet little battling prince.

Not having parents around meant that I was raised by my grandparents on both sides of the family quite a lot.

If you were or are lucky enough to be raised by your grandparents, you would know how hard it is later to slowly watch them leave this planet. I learnt so much from all my grandparents.

I do not remember my mum's dad, Pa Jim, as much as the others because he passed away when I was twelve. I do remember that the entire side of my mum's family was so saddened by his loss and I felt the pain of my mum for a very long time after his death. Watching family videos and seeing Pa Jim, I can still feel the power of his love and the role he played in that side of the family. So much respect was there and losing him I watched a piece of my mum die too.

I also watched my Nanny Fae struggle for years with her mental health. Nanny spent months in a rehabilitation centre in the hospital when Pa first passed. Imagine loving someone so much that when they pass, a piece of you passes away too. That's what happened with Nanny, but not just a piece of her: I feel like an entire half of her went away. It was so frightening to watch the strongest woman in our family lose her mind.

Thankfully, through the power of prayer and love and absolute determination, Nanny Fae came back to us. After months of therapy, love, and shock treatment, she came back.

I don't remember this overly much because I was young, but I do remember the feeling. I have always been such a deep feeler. I sometimes think that I may be very sensitive to people's energies and I feel everyone's pain a little too deeply, so that I hold it in my body and heart not knowing what to do with all this feeling.

I got that from my Nanny Fae, for sure. Her heart was deeper than the ocean. She was just so important to me – there's a whole chapter about her in this book – and when we lost her last year … well, you'll read about that too.

My middle brother, Bradley, and I had that many epic camping trips with our dad's father, Poppy Ted, who also passed away in 2018. Camping with your poppy and your dad is a serious must-do.

I was never a fancy kid. We never had fancy holidays. I didn't go on a plane until I was sixteen and that was to Sydney with one of my best friends at the time. Growing up our holidays were footy trips and camping trips with Poppy. We would learn about all the different types of birds and drink condensed milk out of those tubes when my dad wasn't looking.

Dad was adamant about us being these insanely healthy children. We had to smash an apple before we ever had any junk food. That doesn't sound like torture, but it is when you are holidaying with bulk children who are allowed to smash chippies and poppers and you can't leave your room until you eat your apple a day – because apparently it keeps the doctor away. Our dad was a goddamn OCD freak when it came to eating a piece of fruit a day and cleaning our teeth.

I tell ya what: an apple a day certainly does not keep the doctor away and that is a fact. I smashed that many apples during my childhood and I was constantly on antibiotics. So throw that big ol' myth right in the bin along with 'sticks and stones will break my bones but words will never hurt me'. Also a big fat lie. People's words can really mess with your head. Especially as a kid. Whoever made up those two sayings needs a good talking-to. Words can hurt you for a lifetime. I've broken four bones and I have never been messed up over that. But remember this ... words of others are choices. You choose whether or not you want to hold on to them. If they don't serve your greatest self, then set that toxic shit free. You're worth it!

CHAPTER 3

Childhood: Part 2

Something pretty B-grade-movie-like happened to me when I was a little girl.

I think I was around seven years old. My Nanna Kent took me out for lunch at the ol' Sunshine Plaza on the Sunshine Coast, where we lived.

Nan told me that we would be meeting a friend of hers there. I did not think anything of it – I was just excited to be with my Nanna smashing some food and I'd probably get a present because I was a bit of a spoilt brat – being the first grandchild on the Kent side of the family meant that Nan and Poppy Ted spoiled me rotten.

We got to lunch and this young lady was there. I was too little to understand age but I do remember thinking she was a lot younger than my Nan (she would have been about eighteen or so).

I remember getting this feeling of complete admiration for this young lady I'd just met. We talked a lot and she told me she loved apes – and now I look back and realise that this is what started my obsession with wanting to rescue the gorillas, following in the footsteps of my queen Dian Fossey. That and how much I loved the movie *Gorillas in the Mist*.

I remember leaving that lunch feeling chuffed that I had made such a nice friend. We started to be pen pals. This lady would write to me and put little mermaid stickers all over the letters she sent me. Cue my obsession with mermaids.

A while later we lost touch and I guess I must have just let that go, but I often thought of her and asked Mum or Nan where she was and what she was up to. And instead of calling her 'she' how about we refer to her as Mermaid. (I don't want to say her name for privacy reasons.)

About five years on, when I was around twelve years old, I found out that this ape-loving, mermaid-sticker queen was my half-sister! Dad was seventeen when she was born.

My heart felt funny. I knew there was something different about her and, looking back, it makes sense that I remember her so vividly. That lunch with her and Nan stuck out in my mind like a sore thumb and at the time I had no idea why.

I was so happy to find out that I had a sister – but I was also sad because, being young, I started thinking silly thoughts like, *I am not my dad's first little girl*, and I wasn't Nan and Poppy's first little princess.

It also made me sad that Dad did not see his daughter. After hearing the entire story I found out why they are not in contact, and I completely respect the decision that was made by my dad and Mermaid's mum at the time. They were so young and life happens. Again, that side of this story is not my story to tell; I can only share the story through my thoughts and experience of it all.

I often wondered why we could not be sisters like everyone else and was sad that it was such a big secret kept for so many years, but again I had to respect the decision made by two people in such a vulnerable position.

I do love that nowadays these kinds of situations are so common. You can have brothers and sisters to Mummy's new girlfriend or Daddy's new boyfriend and Mummy and Daddy are still good friends even though they are no longer together or enjoy the same gender like they used to. I call it the modern family and I love it.

People are so much more open to talking about relationships that did not work and sharing new families with old families. I understand that back then it wasn't as acceptable, so it must have been hard for my dad and Mermaid's mum.

I met with Mermaid again. Finally, after all those years, we caught up and she was just as fabulous as I remembered her when I was a wee lass. I hope to get to know her and her beautiful family, because technically I am an aunty! I would love to get to know my nephews and niece.

Reconnecting with good souls, whether it be a long-lost sister or a friend, is just the bee's knees. The feeling of connection is pure and real.

Everyone has secrets and by no means is any family perfect. We are all a bit wild and have our hectic hardships. Find some solace in knowing you are not alone. I could write an entire book on how nutso my family is. Maybe not an entire book, but I reckon at least half a book. Some of it would be cringe but the majority would be bulk laugh-out-loud moments and some real heart-string pullers. That's what family life is all about. Be open, share your story and embrace it.

CHAPTER 4

School

I loved, loved, loved school. I believe there were probably times that I didn't, but when I think about it right now, I just loved it.

In primary school I was queen of the nerds. I was friends with everyone. I wanted to be friends with everyone. I'm not sure what anybody really thought of me. I just know that I tried my hardest to be everyone's best friend because I'm such a people pleaser, and I remember having the best friends.

I love to learn, and I was always the teacher's pet. Now I remember what I was like then and I think, *Oh my god, what a pet.* People must have thought I was such a goody-two-shoes. And I was – I'll fully admit that. I'm not denying that at all.

But I adored primary school. I feel like maybe it was a bit of an escape for me too, growing up with a brother who was unwell and parents who weren't around as much when I first started school. Mum missed my first day and she was away a lot during my first year of school with Josh being so sick.

So I usually had my grandparents dropping me off and picking me up, which I loved. But obviously I missed my mum because we were so close, and then she was kind of taken from me by this new child that I didn't really even know yet. When you're little, of course, you don't understand why certain things are happening. You think, *Who is this evil baby that's coming? Taking my mother from me.* But as I grew up, I totally understood that that wasn't the case at all.

Mothers do whatever they can for their newborn babies and mothers continue to do whatever they can pretty much for their child's entire existence.

Back to primary school: I was actually school captain of Stella Maris Catholic School in 2002, when I was twelve years old. That meant I had to get up and do public speaking; being an anxious person, I can't even believe now that I could do it, but I did.

It was probably really good for me to get that experience in young. Maybe I got a taste for it and that's why I continued to do it throughout my life. Until this day I get nervous, but I can still stand up and talk in front of people and you probably wouldn't even be able to tell that I'm crapping myself. I'm quite a good pretender. Fake it until you make it, y'all!

I really enjoyed friendship groups in primary school. I enjoyed being school captain. I enjoyed always trying to be the best at everything. I don't remember a lot of fights, but I do remember different friends coming into the group and other friends being a little bit funny about it. But because I wanted everyone to be friends with everyone, I would just let anyone into the group.

Of course, there was a popular group that we weren't a part of. We were the second popular group. You know, if all the cool boys had dated everyone from the popular group they would start dating our group because we were next in line … It's funny to look back and realise that's how we thought.

I dated one of the most popular boys in school and everybody was a little bit confused as to why he was dating me because I was such a goody-goody, but it was probs because I started getting boobs at the age of eleven and I was classified as tall and had long blonde hair and I was super tan and super good at all my schoolwork. All the teachers loved me. Maybe he thought, *Ooh, this chick's got boobs – she'll put out*. But my god was he wrong. Little did he know I spent my evenings praying with my grandmother.

The last thing on my mind in primary school was kissing boys, although I had started to like them.

Actually, I always liked boys. I used to get big crushes, but I was so nervous and I would never tell them. I always crushed out hard even from as young as Year One, and I remember having a crush on this guy at that age.

I adored high school too, even if there were some struggles. I was getting to know my anxiety, and my eating disorder kicked in when I was fourteen – I'll tell you more about that later. But I still loved high school.

In Year Eight and Year Nine I was naughty because I got quite a lot of attention and had an older sister-figure at school, and that might have inspired me to push the boundaries a bit. I wasn't smoking ciggies on campus or hooking up with boys in toilets or whatever. My version of naughty was talking back to teachers, and for a while I didn't do my homework, and was more interested in boys than school work.

By Year Ten, though, I was all about the study again. Books before boys! I wanted a really good OP (that's Overall Positions – the Queensland equivalent of your ATAR) so I could go to uni.

I have always had a creative mind. I've never been a businessy or mathematically blessed human. Much to my father's dismay. Growing up my freakin' father would have me up night after night doing D.A.D.

Mentalese. What is that, you ask? It's where I would spend hours doing maths sums, and if I got them wrong I probs didn't get dessert or was not allowed to watch *Home and Away* or something. It was actual mental torture for someone who just wanted to make up poetry or dress up my little brothers by putting my mum's stockings over their heads so we could all have really long hair like Pocahontas.

I never really asked my dad why he wanted me to nail the whole maths thing, but I guess it was because he was so good at it that he wanted me to be too. Or maybe it was because I was quite good at all the other subjects so he had to have me at least try to be good at maths. Or maybe it was a bonding session turned incredibly wrong.

Whatever it was, I bloody hated it. The only maths I need in my life is counting them dollar bills that I don't even have yet. Best believe they are comin', though.

Even if I had maths torture at home, I had a great group of friends at school. We were always hanging out with each other and we didn't have many fights. I was really blessed in that department.

There was the occasional wanker who needed to start a fight. But when any of us think about that kind of behaviour from our high school years, it's good to remember that when you're a teenager your hormones are on fire and you really shouldn't hold resentment or judgement towards people and how they acted in high school. You never know what is going on at home for them, and in combination with the hormones it can make people behave not at their best.

People never had any idea how much I was struggling at home or how intense my eating disorder was, because I always played a different character at school. So if you have pain from your high school years, maybe don't hold on to too much of it because a lot of people are struggling and they don't know what to do with their emotions. And if they're getting treated dreadfully at home, they usually take it out on people at school. They take it out on the weakest link, and that is never going to be the person who's actually hurting them in the first place. Not that I'm saying that's the answer. In my eyes, bullying is one of the worst things in the world to happen to children. It's just awful.

So if it happened to you, just try your very best to forgive. Never forget, though, because of course you can't forget. If you've been bullied it is probably embedded and held in places in your body that you haven't even discovered yet. But definitely forgive.

Don't do it for them – do it for yourself. If you forgive you're releasing that power they hold over you. Why would you want to waste your energy on somebody you're so angry with? If you forgive them, you are showing your strength and character, that you can move on from a stage in your life when you were so hurt. So I think it's more power to you, not for them.

CHAPTER 5

Nanny Fae

I want to devote a whole chapter to my Nanny Fae, even though it's so hard to put such a person in to words. But she was incredibly special to me, and a huge part of my life for so many years.

The main thing I remember about Nanny Fae was that she was the person who was there for us the most while Mum was in hospital looking after Josh and Dad obviously had to work to keep the family funds coming in, so we could afford to do all our sports and things. (That is quite traditional in Queensland society – if you're not doing all the sports, people wig out.)

Nanny and I would have sleepovers. I had a single bed and another single bed that pulled out underneath and she'd sleep on that.

We were both terrible sleepers. She suffered sleep problems her entire life. I think that's a gene that was passed on to my mum and then to me as well; we're all pretty dreadful sleepers.

Nanny and I would have big talks before I fell asleep and she would give me fairy dust. We would sprinkle fairy dust under our pillows and we would say a prayer. Growing up very Catholic, I was a big pray-er as a child. I could not sleep unless I prayed to God and I had to do 'In the name of the father, son and Holy Spirit, Amen' with the actions. I even remember having sleepovers at friends' houses where I would hope they were asleep because I'd have to quickly do the actions. I would hope they wouldn't see me but if I didn't do them my anxiety and my guilt would be almost off the charts. I had to pray otherwise I couldn't switch off.

Not that my Nanny ever forced me into praying – it was a ritual for both of us. Once I grew up I stopped doing it, though. I'm not sure why, but maybe it was because I loved praying with her and once I wasn't living near her anymore it didn't feel the same.

Both of my grandmothers were around a lot when I was young but I remember Nanny Fae, my mum's mum, giving me more spiritually and mentally. Nanna Kent spoilt me more; she was always dressing me up and taking me to the shops and buying me things, and I'd go on more adventures with the Kent grandparents because Poppy Ted would take us camping and to McDonald's, and he was always getting us treats and telling us jokes. Nanny Fae and Pa Jim were more of the sensible ones that I would get deep with. I was just so lucky to have them all. I had such respect for my grandparents that it's indescribable; I guess this is because they were like second parents to me.

We always said about Nanny Fae that she had a direct line to God. We always left our problems with her and she would pray about them. And then the next day it was almost as if the problems didn't seem as big. Nanny held prayer groups – she would ask the whole retirement village where she lived to pray for her family and they would do it.

Every single person who met Nanny got the same feeling about her. If my friends met her they'd say, 'Whoa, your nan's just really different, isn't she?'

It was almost as if she was an actual angel. I think that's why she felt so deeply and couldn't switch off – I think she was always receiving messages from a higher power and angels, so her mind was just constantly going. And her kind heart was always working overtime.

That's why it eventually clocked out. It had had enough, working nonstop for eighty-four years, creating magic and healing people. It was just her time to let go and not have to look after people anymore.

Whenever there were troubles in the family, I went to Nanny's and we had massive talks. About how my heart was broken that my mum and dad were just not treating each other right. About how much I wanted my mum to leave my dad and do her own thing. Or how I just wanted my dad to get help and to truly know his worth.

Nanny would only have to look at me and I could just feel what she was thinking, and she'd hold my hands and we'd close our eyes and pray. Throughout my life Nanny and I did so much praying together, which is funny because as I mentioned I don't pray anymore. But I do speak to the universe quite a lot and I speak to her. She gave me so much faith in a higher power. And her love was so intense that it was almost overwhelming.

The simplest explanation for our relationship is that we shared a connection. I think some people are just soul mates. Nanny Fae was my soul mate and she still is my soul mate.

One of the most beautiful things now is that I receive signs from her all the time. If I'm in a funk, I'll pause. Then I'll take three deep breaths. And I'll say something like, 'Tell me what I need to do. Tell me what you want me to see or what you want me to hear.'

The answer won't come straightaway. But then a little bit later on something will happen. I might help someone out; it could be an older lady and she'll turn around and she'll be wearing a big blue butterfly brooch. The blue butterfly – or any butterfly – is Nanny's symbol because she loved butterflies so much. She had little butterfly stickers on everything. She had old butterfly ornaments all through her house. So now whenever we see a butterfly, we know it's her.

Butterflies aren't super common to see in Queensland – mainly we get moths. So when I see a butterfly I think, *That's my spirit angel. She is reaching out.*

Her signs always seem to pop up at the right time, or I'll get a feeling – like I'll get shivers down my spine – and I'll know that's Nanny telling me to get out of my head and into my body, or that she's here whenever I need her.

All I have to do is ask for her and she will show me the way. She'll give me the answers.

I am so lucky to have so many memories of my childhood spent with all my grandparents, but I have such a special place in my heart for Nanny Fae. It's a connection. It's a feeling. I don't think words will ever do it justice. I just know. And when you know, you know. If you don't know or feel your angels yet, or have never prayed to a higher power before and you don't know where to begin, please know that my Nanny Fae is where you can start. Never judging, always listening. You are never alone. Give it a go. I guarantee she is listening.

CHAPTER 6

Family

Some people say you can choose your friends but you can't choose your family. However, I believe we pick our family. The day we win that race – the conception race – we have picked our family. The universe was saying, 'Yep, you won because this is where you need to learn your lessons.' That's true even if you've had a shit-house upbringing and your mother or father are not like your friends' parents, and you think, *Why me?*

I believe that somewhere, eventually, down the track you will realise why.

Maybe your dad drank and gambled a lot and didn't show you a lot of that love you craved from a male figure. Maybe your mum doesn't know how to take care of herself and you sometimes resent her for not putting herself first, so because you have never seen a strong woman figure that's why you think you are weak and don't have a lot of self-love.

This is sad – don't get me wrong – and my heart goes out to you, but have you ever thought that maybe you had to experience that with your dad because now you have learnt that because of him you really know how to enjoy life? You don't want to waste your life drinking and gambling and working a job you don't really love to do but which you've done because 'society' made you feel like you had to be the provider. Now you can see this way of living and say, 'No, I want more for myself. And I want to love myself and stand up for what I believe.'

Maybe your mother didn't love herself, and didn't – or couldn't – stand up for herself, and it affected you so much that now you know how painful it can be, so you don't want to do that to yourself or to your kids.

Family are here to teach us lessons and for us to learn from them what we want more or less of. I know it can be really hard to believe that sometimes, especially when things are tough, but that doesn't make it less true.

I love my family so hard out. I love them so much I feel we share the same heart – me, Nanny Fae and Mum definitely did. And even though sometimes I don't agree with how members of my family have lived and how they didn't stand up for themselves enough, without them I never would have this kind, precious heart that I have that feels deeply for so many things.

How blessed I am to have that experience. To be so close to my family that if something happens to one of us, we all feel it as if it has happened to us personally.

I'm not here to rub in how lucky I am with the family I got – because believe-you-me there have been some horrendous times that I still feel like I can't open up about because I am still coming to terms with how I relate to what happened.

If you don't have that love I have with my family, don't be alarmed! Because you can create your own family. Even though I was blessed with loving my immediate family so much, I also created my own family as I got older. I did this within different friendship circles.

My friends are my family. My pack of rescue dogs over the years were my family. You can even meet your soul mate and start your own family. Or just create your own soul mates – whatever or whoever you want that to be.

You don't have to stick by the traditional family. What even is tradition anymore? How lucky we are to live in a world where we can create our own magic more so than ever. Yes, we can still be judged by not fitting in with the norm, but many of us just seem to give less f*cks. Good on us.

I like to talk about 'magic moments'. Magic moments are when you finally realise why you do the things you do in life and why certain things happen but at the time you just can't work out why. A magic moment in my family – or a silver lining, as some like to call it – is that I had a very unwell baby brother while I was growing up.

That doesn't sound like a magic moment or something to be grateful for, but hear me out.

My brother was born with kidney failure and many other complications. This meant that within those first few years of his beautiful little baby life, my mum and dad and Josh were in and out of hospital a lot, so I was partly raised by my grandparents. That's the magic moment. Without them I never would be who I am or have had the respect that I did for those magical beings who created my parents.

My baby brother Josh was then diagnosed with Asperger's (now called autism spectrum) and a chromosome abnormality called supernumerary ring chromosome 1, which is a tiny extra part of a chromosome in all or some of the cells of the body.

Meet Joshua – he's now my 24-year-old big (but little) baby brother who has been a fighter from the day he was born.

While we were growing up we had no idea that Josh had Asperger's – he wasn't diagnosed until he was eleven years old, and it wasn't until he was fifteen that we found out that he had supernumerary ring chromosome 1.

This diagnosis was like a giant light bulb for my family. Josh had been in and out of hospital with kidney damage resulting in a ureterostomy; he also had low muscle tone and problems with fine and gross motor skills, and affected and delayed intellectual development and social skills, which I guess is a.k.a. being on the spectrum.

Ahhh, I don't think I breathed when I read all that back to myself out loud.

Josh was – is – unique, but to be honest my entire family was/is unique in their own little ways.

All the signs of Josh having Asperger's weren't really obvious to us; we just figured that because he was in and out of hospital so much as a baby he was taking a little longer to play catch-up, so to speak.

Growing up, Josh often was in his own little world. He would escape into his room and listen to music over and over again. He still does.

Josh also came out as gay when he was about sixteen. We kind of already knew because he spent a lot of time in my room going through my wardrobe, trying on my high-heeled boots, dressing up in costumes and making us refer to him as Jessica Alba or Angelina Jolie. It's safe to say that referring to himself as those two dreamboats meant he didn't lack confidence. Aim high, brother, aim high!

While we are on this topic: looking back, I realise even more now just how amazing my friends were. We often had to pause our game-playing or stop our gossiping because Josh – I mean, Jessica Alba – had spent the last hour rehearsing for a concert that we didn't ask for.

He would walk in wearing my knee-high boots and my tiny little sparkly-gold Kylie Minogue dance pants with no top and a cape, and we would watch him perform 'These Boots Were Made for Walking' – the Jessica Simpson version.

My friends didn't even flinch, and I sure as shit didn't because I was so used to it, but I often thought, *Oh, I wonder if this weirds my friends out* – and it just didn't. Or if it did they certainly didn't show it.

And this isn't now, in 2019, when being super flamboyant and a bit cray are more accepted. This was late 1990s/early 2000s when mental health wasn't overly talked about. Actually, it wasn't talked about at all on the ol' Sunny Coast.

My friends would clap and say, 'Cute boots, Josh,' (sometimes the boots were theirs and he'd pinched them from my room when we weren't looking) and they were just so cavalier about it. For those friends who are reading this: thank you. You know who you are and I am forever grateful for how much you accepted my little soul mate of a brother.

I feel that having this unique set-up – not only Josh but spending so much time with my grandparents – made me accepting of everyone and everything. Don't get me wrong: I can be incredibly judgemental in my delivery with certain things, but it's generally for a laugh, and if you need me and when it comes down to it, I would never have a serious judgement that changes my opinion of the way those dear to me choose to live their lives.

Growing up with a brother who was very eccentric was magical, but that wasn't always the case. I was jealous as all hell of him when I was a little lass.

Josh would absolutely lose his shit if the attention wasn't on him, and if someone else was opening presents, he couldn't understand why.

I remember being patient with Josh, but after binge-watching old family videos while I was back in my hometown of the Sunshine Coast recently, I could see little Angie was always trying to pull him aside and explain to him why he couldn't act out like this, and to give others a go.

Sometimes you can even see me pinching his arm when he refused to pose properly for a family photo.

Nine-year-old Angie wanted everything perfect, while four-year-old Josh wanted to chuck up the deuces.

I look back now and think, *Good on him, doin' his own thang.*

Growing up, I would say Josh was allowed to break all the rules, while my other brother Bradley and I were on quite a tight leash. I was very jealous of the attention Josh received, but at the same time I also felt like he was always by my side.

Wearing my knee-high boots and little dancing costumes that wouldn't fit me no more, and all my friends really accepted him. This I am truly grateful for.

Looking back on this makes me remember how much my friends never made us, or Josh, feel weird about how we acted at home.

There is this one time, though, that really has made quite the dent in my heart.

Josh came to visit me, while I was living in Sydney, for a few days. We were so excited because Josh doesn't really get the chance to jet off anywhere, and people do tend to bail on his plans, which is another thing that breaks my heart.

So coming to Sydney was a big deal for this small-town guy.

We went to a bunch of gay clubs, dancing and drinking; it's in these types of venues where we feel right at home.

One night a friend and I took him to the eastern suburbs of Sydney, which turned out to be a BIG mistake. Josh was refused entry in not one but two places, with the bouncers saying he was drunk (I won't name names, but if they ever read this they know who they are and karma is a good friend of mine).

One security guy was willing to come to the side with me, so I could explain that Josh has Asperger's and a chromosome abnormality that makes him look that way all the time, as they were accusing him of looking too drunk.

In fact, he was sober and *I* was drunk – so why wasn't I refused entry?

This one security guard was understanding enough to let him in and he even apologised.

I understand they were just doing their jobs but I felt sick that I even had to reveal my brother's details to them after I had already explained that he had a medical condition and was not drunk.

The second place was not quite as friendly, to put it nicely. They refused to talk to me until I asked to see the manager. The manager went on to say that Josh had to carry a doctor's certificate explaining his medical history, because he looked drunk and they were only going off what he looked like.

I was mortified. Josh had to stand there and listen to this.

After a lot of toing and froing, my friend got involved and I heard the manager say to my friend, 'Fine, her and her special needs brother can come in.'

Obviously we didn't go in after that. I put Josh in a cab and we went home.

The next day I wrote a status update on the *Gogglebox* Angie and Yvie Facebook page, and only then was I contacted by the boss saying how completely sorry he was and that we should come back for VIP service. No thanks, mate, I'd rather cheese grate my nipples than sit there and be treated like I am a VIP when the other day we weren't even worthy enough to step foot in your fancy establishment.

I think at the time I was boozy AF and had a lot to say, but when approached sober I was willing to listen to their poor-as-piss apology and guilt offer even if I wouldn't take them up on it.

I am, however, glad that I removed myself and my brother from the situation and got us home instead of carrying on too much (homegirl can really let loose when you speak shit about her friends or family), and instead of squealing too hardcore I put on my big gal boots and took it to social media, where I felt I could express my pain and our side of the story without being publicly humiliated (again).

There have been a lot of situations like this. Josh was bullied throughout his high school life. There were times I wanted to get in there like a bull in a china shop and have Josh's back ... but we can't baby our little bros forever and I don't want to step in the way of the universe's idea of karma.

Sometimes we just need to be patient and know that the universe strikes at the time that is right. We don't need to do the dirty work.

I think there's something quite comforting in knowing that everyone is on their own path and has their own stories, so each of us handles family situations differently to the next person.

I do know one thing: people who treat others badly are generally very unhappy with themselves.

I feel blessed in some degree that Josh doesn't really take on any of the negative dross too much. If he gets hurt, he kind of just bitches about it and then goes into his room and plays one of his 1000 albums and recites every single word to every single song and then comes out as fresh as a daisy.

Routine and music are a big thing for Josh (and taking selfies at every place he ever goes, sometimes even the toilet). Without these routines Josh does act out. But don't we all?

Life is tough enough as is, so instead of judging why don't we bloody listen and put ourselves in other people's shoes? And if you do make a mistake and say something you shouldn't – which god knows we all do – then be big enough to acknowledge it and apologise.

We all have our struggles, that's for damn sure, but knowing that you're not alone offers some comfort. Everyone's got their own stuff going on and you really never know what goes on behind closed doors.

CHAPTER 7

Loss

For the last couple of years I have spent the majority of my time thinking about anything and everything else so I did not have to think about how completely unhappy I was.

I didn't have a home base for a long time. I was house sitting and pet sitting and living out of my car while I moved between Sydney and London.

Working as a nanny, as a carer for people with a disability, filming for a television show where I felt I had to act like I was fine and loving life so the rest of Australia could laugh along with me once a week.

Deep down I was on struggle street.

I look back now and think that I made life harder for myself so I had a reason to struggle and I didn't have to admit that I was just unhappy with my current set-up – which was ultimately something I had created for myself.

If I looked busy, then I could just say I was stressed and that was why I was not really coping.

Gogglebox was filming and I had to work so I could afford to live in Sydney, but I had no home base because I could not afford rent due to flying back to the Sunshine Coast so often. I was flying home for some very special family events, such as cousins' and uncles' birthday milestones, and I also had amazing new opportunities in local radio.

But I was mostly going back so often because I had a lot of loss in my life that year. I flew home when my grandfather, Poppy Ted, passed away. I then flew home to look after my Nanny Fae, who had become unwell with what we thought was severe hip pain. Eventually it led to her depression coming back.

I stayed for a week to help Nanny settle back into a routine when she got out of hospital, since she was struggling so badly with pain and with seeing the light again. I would try to motivate her to get out of bed, get dressed and have breakfast, and then we would try to spend the day praying and thinking of all the beautiful things she could do when she was fighting fit again.

A couple of months later I flew home to the Sunshine Coast for a gig on breakfast radio. One morning, after I finished work for the day, I was driving to Nanny's to take her out for brunch. I called her but she didn't answer so I figured that she must be out on the porch with a support worker or with one of her many beautiful visitors.

A bit later I called again – still no answer. This wasn't like her at all.

Maybe she was having a slow start to the morning and couldn't get to the phone quick enough due to her painful hip?

So I drove to her house anyway. When I arrived there was a police car out the front as well as the nurse's car. I thought to myself, *Oh no, there has been a robbery in the retirement village.*

I got out of my car and as I was walking to Nanny's house I noticed all her dear friends and neighbours out the front.

'Hello,' I said, and continued walking to the front door.

'Are you okay?' one of the ladies called out to me.

'Yes, of course!' I said. 'I'm just picking up Nanny to take her out for brunch.'

The lady's face fell.

'Angie,' she said, 'your Nanny has passed away.'

I felt like everything was in slow motion, like my brain was trying to work out what she'd said. Then I screamed and fell onto the road. It was just like you see in the movies.

You never know how you're going to react until you are going through something so intense. I had no control over my body – it was trembling and shaking and I couldn't stand up. I sobbed so much that my eyes were so watery I couldn't even see my hands in front of me.

'Maybe you heard wrong,' I said to Nanny's friends, because I didn't want it to be true. 'Maybe she's just sleeping.'

But the looks on their faces told me the truth.

'I'll go in and wake her up,' I said, still refusing to believe it.

When the policeman hurried out of Nanny's house, picked me up off the road and put me on a seat in the garage, it started to sink in. And then I couldn't breathe. But I wasn't alone – I was surrounded by real-life angels, my Nanny Fae's beloved friends.

The nurse came out to the garage and told me what had happened that morning. Although my head was spinning and I could hardly understand what she said, I do remember her saying that Nanny closed her eyes and went to sleep. It was a very peaceful death.

Nanny's heart had stopped. From all the pain, from all the different medications, from trying so hard to get better for us, her brave heart finally gave up. So unexpectedly, so devastating.

The nurse asked me if I wanted to go in and see Nanny, but I waited for my mum and aunty to arrive. My mum was a mess. She lived for her mother; so did my aunty. They were soul mates.

We all went in together and there she was on the floor in the living room. Our angel. Cold and finally resting. She had struggled with sleep her whole life, so to see her there completely asleep did bring some peace to us all. Especially after the last few months of me, my mum and aunty trying to get Nanny back on her feet. Her struggle had ended at last.

My mum screamed and sobbed, and we just sat around Nanny's lifeless body until they came to take her away from her home. The beautiful little home in Bli Bli where we'd spent so many happy times.

Afterwards I was so angry. Why did she die the morning I was taking her for brunch? Why did she die at all? Why did the universe not allow us to just enjoy those last six months instead of forcing her to get into this routine of thinking she would get better?

The biggest question was: *Why did you do this to my mum?* I really did not see how my mum would cope without her mum. I still don't believe she has completely mourned Nanny as we have been so busy and distracted with the madness of my crazy life since the passing of Nanny.

It has taken me quite some time to forgive the universe for all these unanswered questions.

But thanks to going into the jungle for *I'm a Celebrity ... Get Me Out of Here!* (I'll tell you more about that later) and getting to know myself again, and my new-found love for kinesiology and going back to seeing a naturopath, I am slowly letting go of my resentment.

I have also felt guilty being so angry at the universe. How dare I question the power of the universe and the universe's plans? When your heart is broken, though, it is quite hard not to ask questions and be so angry. But I am getting there. Baby steps.

After Nanny died, I still had to face my own life. Not having a home in Sydney and going back to film *Gogglebox* was hard. I felt fake because really my heart was completely broken, but I had a responsibility to finish that last season we did of *Gogglebox*. I did not want to let my TV family down.

Not having a safe place to call home made it even harder. I was no longer living with Yvie so while I was in Sydney I was constantly moving from house sitting strangers' homes to sleeping on friends' couches.

Sometimes I would be so overwhelmed I would sleep in my car during the day down by the water somewhere.

If I had a dollar for how many times I drove somewhere trying to get away from people, pulled over and just cried and cried until I eventually fell asleep, woke up again to go to work or wait for someone to get home so I could sleep on their couch, I wouldn't be rich but I would have more than a handful of dollars, that's for sure.

So, yes, 2018 was quite the clusterf*ck of sorrow. I didn't want to be a burden on these beautiful people who would let me stay in their homes but sometimes I just did not want to talk to anyone.

I couldn't really sleep at night because that's when my mind would run like wildfire. Plus, I was in so many strange houses that my body was uncomfortable and anxious. My appetite was nonexistent too.

I bet if I was someone else watching that last season of *Gogglebox* that Yvie and I were in, I wouldn't be able to tell how much I was suffering. But Sydney was well and truly giving me all the signs that it was done with me for now. I needed to get home and be with my mumma, and that I did.

•

With all that being blurted out, I would firstly like to say that I feel this instant weight lifted off my shoulders – and it is also safe to say that last year was the icing on top of an already very average cake in the self-sabotage department.

I did try to start the year off right. After years of house sitting and living between Sydney and London, I finally decided to settle and get myself into a place I could call home, so I could become more grounded and get this little bod into some kind of healthy routine.

For years I have had the wildest body clock and routine. (Well, actually, my body clock was nonexistent.)

The outcome I hoped to have by being in the one place was that maybe I could get to know myself again and move on from this whirlwind of a life I was addicted to.

I was seeing a few different guys, mainly just to have that attention from the opposite sex. (I am only human, after all.) But I was always keeping these gents at a healthy distance so neither of us could get close enough to catch the feels – because, my god, catching feels was so out of my emotional capability at that point. I was scared shitless of someone really getting to know me and seeing the right mess that I thought I was.

So I finally did it. I got myself this little pad by the harbour in Drummoyne, in Sydney's inner western suburbs. I started seeing this one guy more than the rest of them and felt a little more stable.

Really, though, I was still a bag of nerves about this life I was living. This somewhat normal-ish life.

I gave it all up within three months because that commitment was far too real. I was going home so much to look after my Nanny that it just did not feel right to be spending all this money renting a place when I was rarely there. I wanted to spend half my week in Sydney for filming and work, and the other half getting Nanny back on track.

Then BOOM ... There went my stable home: my beautiful Poppy suddenly passed away, the nice fella I was 'kind of seeing' (as I always like to put it so I don't have to admit I actually like someone), well, that ended quicker than it began, and to top it all off I lost Nanny, my real-life angel, unexpectedly. I didn't get to move home to be with her at all.

Everything I was hoping would pan out did the exact damn opposite. I couldn't eat, couldn't sleep, couldn't even think past the fact I had to attend the funeral of my favourite person in the world.

Another end came when my friend Yvie and I gave up the television show we were on for four years, and I packed up my eight-year life in Sydney and moved home to be closer to my family after all the loss of 2018. Whattamess!

So why did I tell you this little sad sack of a tale? Because I believe that if I hadn't experienced that year, that heartbreak, all that loss, then I wouldn't be where I am.

Why is where I am so good? Well, I finally understand why things happen the way they do. In some weird way I needed that shit-fight to happen in order to find clarity. When I accepted and let go of all these horrible feels and outlooks I had created in my little wild mind, all these amazing opportunities started coming my way.

Without feeling that heartbreak, I would not have known what real love felt like.

When you lose someone you love so much, the pain is unbearable – but now I think there's no way in the world I wouldn't want to love my Nanny as much as I did. That love was pure and real and filled up my soul!

So you have to accept the pain to appreciate the love. I wouldn't avoid that pain, because that means I would have to dull down the love I received and gave to her. And that is something that will never happen.

CHAPTER 8

Self Care

Having a career is important to me – but nowhere near as important as having a solid relationship with myself and using what I have to help others have solid relationships with themselves too.

Over the past few years I came to realise that I didn't love myself at all. These days, there is nothing more rewarding to me than knowing I have made someone feel better about themselves, put a smile on their face or helped them through a hard time. What is more fulfilling and beautiful than that?

I think the time I realised that I needed to love myself and get to know myself – before becoming this person who wants to help everyone – was during that Saturn Return period I mentioned earlier.

I had what I like to now call a spiritual awakening, a.k.a. probably more like a nervous breakdown. Brené Brown (amazing woman, by the way – if you have not checked out her stuff do so STAT) calls it a spiritual awakening, so I am sticking with that.

To keep myself grounded I started practising mindfulness and meditation more, and journalling. I did a lot of research on mental health and wanted to understand it.

I have recently started having kinesiology sessions, and instead of drowning my problems in one too many wines, I am questioning myself, opening up, learning to be vulnerable and putting me first.

Every day right now is so different to the next, so it has been quite hard to have a solid routine, but I do try to exercise five times a week and during that exercise time I really only focus on the activity in front of me. On staying as present as possible.

I used to journal a lot, which I also highly recommend. Writing down my thoughts for myself helps me to get them clear. Though since starting to write this book I have not journalled as much as I used to – this book has become somewhat like a journal!

Each week I will try to have a kinesiology appointment or an energy healing session. If you are lucky enough to have found beautiful soul teachers, after each session they will send you a list of what you discussed through each appointment and from there you can work on those elements, whether that be breathing exercises, feeling where you hold the pain in your body, or knowing why you feel a certain way about something you have been holding on to and then handing it over to the universe.

I also spend more time now listening to my body instead of my wild mind. So when I can I will book in for a Bowen therapy session or a massage to treat and thank my body for getting me through yet another week.

How strong and dedicated our bodies are to us – even though we treat them like shit a lot of the time, they still seem to forgive and give us another chance to treat them better. Bless our bodies' little cotton socks. They truly are troopers.

CHAPTER 9

A Trip Down Mental Health Lane

One thing that is super important to me – and I believe everyone should feel safe to talk about this – is mental health.

Mental health is a bloody serious subject but it should not be a scary one to open up about. Breaking old thought patterns and habits that we are not benefiting from is hard, but it is so doable!

I love so much how more people are coming out and talking about mental health and their struggles. We all need to help each other and not be afraid to admit when we are not okay!!!

There are so many tips and tricks out there that I hope you are all taking advantage of. I have already given some tips and tricks and will continue to mention others throughout this book whenever they come to mind. Remembering this, though: I am not, by any means, a professional in this area. These are just my tips and tricks that I have trialled on my body over time. So please make sure you always speak with a professional first and do what suits your body, mind and spirit.

We really have no excuse to suffer in silence anymore, though. There are even apps dedicated to mindfulness meditation, anxiety, motivation. Heck, Instagram can change my mood from drab to fab with just one inspirational quote.

I do understand, however, that on some days an Instagram post won't do the trick, and for that there are so many amazing people you can talk to, or read about, or check out on the internet. You can even jump online for a chat if you are still not sure about talking to someone face to face.

I don't want to sound all morbid but at the end of the day we are born and then we are gone. So don't take yourself so seriously. The problem you are having right now, is it really going to matter in five years' time? If the answer is no, then let it go. *For the love of god, let it go.*

There is so much love and laughter to be had. Ain't nobody getting out of here alive. Everything in between is an adventure and a chance to grow!

•

I was reading over a blog I did a few years back when I was living between London and Sydney. I feel I have blocked out that part of my life and kind of only remember it as a hectic period. However, when I read over these blog posts I realised that where I was and what I was experiencing were really getting me ready for every other year of my life since, especially this one. My life has changed so much, but I also feel like it is exactly the same. Same same but different, one could say. As in, I still hang with the same people, I am currently living in my old family home in between projects, I spend most of my time lying low – but a lot has changed for me and it's going to get even more hectic. I feel like I'm the same, I am just happier and have had some magic moments with an even bigger magic moment coming up later this year that could ultimately change my world forever.

So let's read over some of my previous 'magic moments', as I like to call them.

When I look back I can see that I have been way more self-aware than I give myself credit for. After reading these blog posts I am actually quite impressed! That's a message for another time, though: knowing when to give ourselves credit and a big ol' pat on the back. We just don't do that enough.

Okay, so, magic moments, here we go …

They say time flies when you're having fun! People don't often tell you that time also flies when you're moving from house to house, looking after a bunch of different dogs, working day and night, filming every weekend and trying to stay sane. Now *that* kills time like a boss and also causes shingles! (Well, in my case it did.) They also say: *The bad news is that time flies, the good news is you are the pilot!* BUT when you're not a pilot in fine form, that can be quite dangerous.

I feel so much more creative and open when I am away from Sydney. Even though I was running around like a mad woman, back and forth from Sydney to the Sunshine Coast, when I was back home I had a lot of downtime.

During that downtime I would think about all the other things I had to do: where to put all my stuff that I left in storage when I was in London last; what job was I going to do in London next; will these cats and dogs I'm caring for while house sitting like me, or will they feel my crazy anxious vibes and be, like, *Girl bye we are going to turn shit upside down while Mum and Dad are away.* I was a hot mess.

The weird thing is that when I am in Sydney I am too scared to write about what I am feeling or what I am going through. When I am home I feel so inspired that I don't fear the judgement; if anything, I embrace it.

I want to talk about some amazing things that have helped with my mental health. I internally struggle terribly with anxiety and sometimes I can get into a deep depression. I tend to get out of it quite quickly, but the little sucker always seems to sneak back in. Generally my anxiety is at its worst, or my depression will return, when I am run-down, consume too much booze or think I can take on 150 different responsibilities at one time.

I'm forever learning, yet I am still forever putting myself in the same situations. We are funny creatures like that, aren't we?

If you haven't already I highly recommend you get into Deepak Chopra and Oprah Winfrey's '21 Day Meditation' app. It is free and they do them every few months. These little 21-day meditation experiences always seem to come at exactly the right time in my life. Sign up and get amongst the free slices of heaven. I also follow Deepak and the Chopra Center on social media. And it's very first-world of me but their inspirational posts on Instagram have sometimes been lifesavers. They seem to rear their beautiful heads right when I need a little pick-me-up.

Also do yourself a favour and sign up to the Chopra Center email newsletter so you can be notified well in advance as to when the free meditation experiences are coming up. They're true mental lifesavers. They also send amazing emails with links to articles that also always seem to be so fitting for whatever state I'm in.

Another huge spiritual guru of mine is Gabrielle Bernstein. Again, you can follow her on Instagram. She is always posting amazing inspirational quotes, and announcements about when she is doing a free online workshop, or just handing out free meditation practices like it is bloody Christmas up in here. Gabby has a website you can sign up to: gabbybernstein.com. And a Miracle Membership, a fun way to stay consistent with your spiritual practices.

Gabby has also written so many amazing books. My go-to is *The Universe Has Your Back*. I often refer to her work, and read over the book and say her chants and affirmations when I wake up in the morning.

Amongst all these sensational spiritual gurus no one can beat the old faithful: the one, the only, Louise L. Hay. Now, Louise Hay's work really *is* heaven sent.

Even though Louise is no longer with us, her work continues – sign up to louisehay.com. The website also gives out free audiobooks! And the Hay House mobile app is a must. Another go-to book for me is Louise's *You Can Heal Your Life*.

I could sit here and list all the magic of Ms Hay and her story but I believe you should get amongst her work yourself. I promise you will never look back. You're welcome.

CHAPTER 10

The Woo-Woo Stuff

Whenever you're feeling extremely unwell and truly out of sorts – or mental, as I sometimes like to refer to it – make sure you check out what's going on with the planets.

I am telling you, when my mind and life are in a shambles and I feel I am constantly getting tested, I check what the planets are up to, what full or new moon is coming up, etc.

It then makes so much sense to me as to why I am feeling like a wild cat on the hunt to stir shit up at night when my owner is sound asleep. Or whatever mood I'm in.

I got into trusting in the universe and understanding how it affects my mood a few years back. I have always been a spiritual person, growing up with strong religious beliefs in a Catholic household – with my mad Catholic guilt that still comes out often because I am such a people pleaser, just like my mum and Nanny Fae.

I still believe in a higher power and I believe in the legend that is Jesus, but I don't believe the Bible is, well, bible and I certainly don't think this higher power would give a flying f*ck whether or not we are married and to who.

I believe the universe is our higher power, along with Mother Nature and our angels and spirit guides. I also think you should believe in whatever sits well with you.

I got into learning about the planets through Forever Conscious. Tanaaz Chubb, the creator of Forever Conscious, rocks my world and I follow her work. (I highly recommend you also follow Forever Conscious on Facebook and Instagram.) And from there I just expanded my knowledge and noticed whenever there was a full moon, and whatever one it was I would do the practices and the rituals and I would feel lighter and more at ease. More connected to the universe, you could say.

I started writing blogs about all the new moons and the super moons when I was travelling between the UK and Sydney over 2016 and 2017. The whole thing became quite a passion of mine.

Over this past year, though, I kind of stopped. I still try to know when the full moons are coming, just so I am prepared for crazy cat Angie to arise, but I don't get into it as much as I did.

My friends and family would come to me and ask, 'Which moon is this, Angie?' or 'What little ritual do you have planned for the next cycle?' I miss that. So I am going to make a mental note to get back into it. It's important to follow what feels good for you. What fuels your soul.

For those of you who don't believe in the power of a Super Full Moon, it's very much there!

I understand that this may be mumbo-jumbo to some of you, and some others will understand and are so much more sensitive to these types of energies and signals from the environment and what the universe is trying to tell us every day.

We just need to learn to listen. Be still and accept what we can't change, but also be willing to work on the things we can.

I once received a comment from my uncle who was writing to me for Nanny Fae – Nanny's message was that she wanted me to remember that the spirit that I was looking for lives within! Even though we are so hurt and don't understand why, there is always a higher power and our spirit to help us get through. Sometimes we don't have to understand everything. We just need to trust!

This message from Nanny actually made me feel so much more calm and at ease with what was happening to me at that time. I can't really explain why, it just did.

Generally what I was going through then – not really living in any one place, not knowing where I was going to live for the next few months or what job I was going to do, not settled about anything much at all – would cause me quite a bit of anxiety ... but for some reason I had full confidence in the universe. I knew those next few months were going to be tough, but they were going to be an experience and that I would fully embrace it head first. And so it turned out to be.

Part of being able to cope with change and uncertainty was making sure I always looked out for magic moments, because they're everywhere, even if they don't seem like it at the time.

Once I went out for drinks with friends of friends and all of a sudden I had this out-of-body experience. I realised how sensitive I was to certain energies, and I kind of went from being my normal chatty self to really still and silent.

At dinner a few little things started to set me off and I had this overwhelming feeling of dread and emotion. Out of nowhere I felt my past insecurities coming up; I felt picked on and unheard.

This made me realise that even though I have come so far with understanding myself and how my past has played such a part in how I deal with and handle certain things now, I still have so far to go and so much to learn about myself and where I want to be.

A big thing we do as women – and men probably do it too, but I can only speak from a woman's point of view – is that after the age of twenty-five, heading for thirty, you start to compare your life to the lives of those around you.

My life is incredibly different to the majority of my friends'. Some of my nearest and dearest are, like me, approaching thirty years of age and they are up to their second or third child, they own a home, they have been with their partner for five to ten-plus years and a lot of them also have their big gal jobs. Heck, I'm almost thirty and I'm still scratching my head and bumping into things.

But I also think it is important to understand that although we do play a part in achieving what we want out of life, our life is already mapped out for us by the universe (or whatever higher power you believe in). Your actions will dictate your own future, but there is a higher power out there working its magic. Surely us mortal beings can't think we hold all the power?

I am a massive believer in living a divinely guided life after reading books like *The Universe Has Your Back* and following the work of Deepak Chopra and Louise Hay for years. The lessons that they teach help us to relinquish our need to control absolutely everything in our lives and relax into a sense of certainty and faith.

Making the shift from fear to faith at the very least takes the pressure off YOU and only relying on yourself and what you create, and if anything it also gives you the opportunity to believe in something greater than what is simply in front of you. There has to be more to life than this one planet and our own control.

This belief system has helped me for years. People can have their opinions on it but if it makes me feel the feels then I'm going to stick with it. To be love and to spread love – there is really not much better than that.

As you get older you come to appreciate that a lot of what happens is out of your control and that you have to stop attempting to control the things that you can't control. Being a person like me, an Aquarian, on top of being very independent, I've always wanted to do everything my way and by myself. Letting go of control is such a hard thing to do, but it does get easier when you have full faith in whatever you want to believe in.

I believe the universe has my back, and I definitely have manifested what I want.

You have to wake up with a positive outlook and list the things that you want – you can't just wake up and say 'I want to be a doctor or an actress'. You have to put in the hard yards in order to get there. I believe that if it's not the right path for you even though you are so passionate about becoming or being something or someone, you will reach that goal because the universe has seen how hard you worked – but the universe will then lead you down the path that you need to be on.

I have done plenty of things where I thought afterwards, *Why did I do that, what does that have to do with this?* But now, looking back, I see that if I didn't do this or go down that path or meet that particular person, I never would have ended up here, feeling this way and experiencing the things that I am currently experiencing. That in itself is so magical to me.

The most important thing to me is to have my goals and manifest them and also pray to the universe and ask the universe every day: *What do you want me to hear? What do you want me to find out for myself today? Please show me the signs.* And the universe will deliver.

It may not be on your strict time frame or exactly when you thought you needed it, but by golly that sweet, sweet universe will deliver the goods.

The universe is always listening – every little thought you have and every little word you speak, the universe is picking up on those vibes. What you put out you get.

So if you are constantly thinking, *Oh, I can't do this*, or comparing your life to other people's, that's all the universe can see and hear.

Make sure your thoughts match your words and your words match your feelings, and pray to the universe and be grateful. Gratitude is the best damn feeling in the world.

I try to wake up every day and list everything I can think of that I am grateful for! It instantly changes my mood.

It's possible that none of this resonates with you. Maybe you're just not at a point where you need it, or need to hear it. But have you never changed your mind about anything before? After you have some large life experience, your outlook can change on most things you once could comfortably sit on your couch and criticise.

One of my biggest lessons learnt is that life is unpredictable. If we don't grow through what we go through, then how else do we live and learn?

When I lost someone who meant so much to me, so unexpectedly, I realised that I'm not here to f*ck spiders: I am going to take on whatever life has in store. Especially when I know that special someone is the puppeteer behind these life experiences and would never put me in danger.

Why try to be perfect for imperfect people? What a waste of time. No one is perfect. People are always going to have opinions. Refuse to be offended. When people are cruel and judgemental, it's them really revealing themselves. They're telling you what they're lacking and upset with. How you treat those who mistreat you reveals your emotional and spiritual level.

People disliking you isn't necessarily a bad thing. Unless you're an asshole then, yes, I would look into that. But when you are embodying your truest of selves, it creates fear in people who only work from their ego. If you want to grow and move forwards, you have to let go of always wanting to be liked.

Other thoughts I live by:

What's meant to be yours will come.

Remain humble and kind.

Letting things go and letting things flow.

You can't expect people who don't even believe in themselves to believe in you.

And a really big one:

Thoughts have no power over us unless we give them the power. It is a choice. Thoughts are really only words strung into sentences. They have no meaning whatsoever if you don't let them.

CHAPTER 11

Friends

Friendships are so important. Growing up, my friends were my world. Yeah, I went a little boy crazy, thought about boys a lot, had little boyfriends here and there – but my friends were my ride-or-dies.

I've never been through a stage where my friends weren't a massive part of my life. I know some of us go through this stage when we're younger where we tend to say 'my boyfriend is my best friend' – actually, you don't even have to be younger, people of all ages probably do it.

I totally appreciate if your boyfriend is your best friend. I had two amazing boyfriends who were 100 per cent *amongst* my best friends, but they weren't ever my *best* friend. They played big parts in my life, for sure, but the relationships I have with my friends – my girl friends, my guy friends – are so incredibly important.

I think it says a lot about a human when they don't have friends because they have given up their world for their partner. That makes me sad.

If you are as lucky as I have been, your friends have been there for you before you knew what you wanted to be or what you wanted to achieve.

Obviously you make new friends on the way – I've met some amazing friends later in life who I know I was meant to meet.

My school friends, however, have played such a huge part in my life and I couldn't imagine being one of those girls who doesn't have many girl friends. That shit is heartbreaking.

I know girls can be hard work – I am one, so I totally get it – but if you haven't found friends who accept your wild emotional-ride side, you haven't found your clique yet. Manifest that! Because real-deal friendships are what dreams are made of.

I know nowadays it can be harder for girls to make mates. Side track for a minute: you know one thing that really grinds my gears? Us gals have had to compete with men since the beginning of time. Actually, for a good amount of time we weren't even considered in the same league as men, so technically we had no race to compete in – which is even WORSE! And now we have all this equality and this pent-up strength as women to stand up for ourselves and say what we want, show the world what we are made of, and then we go and bloody gang up on each other, fight each other for men?! How ludicrous does that sound? Please tell me it sounds as crazy to you as it does to me.

Sisters, if there is one thing we have in this world it is that magical bond we share as women – and think of the power we have when we all stick together and support one another.

When women stick together and put their heads together, that's when magic happens. That's when the universe is, like, *Hold my damn magic wand: this right here is solid gold*. Watching women communicate and master up plans is pure magic.

So, ladies, there're going to be 1000 other dudes out there for you – there's plenty more fish in the sea. Real friendships last a lifetime and shouldn't be given up for nuttin (that's 'nothing' in Angie slang). They're so beautiful and so pure, and let's just say that if you haven't yet experienced the friendships that I have, your soul sisters are still out there and once you find them they will forever have your back. They aren't going to have a side chick or a 2 a.m. booty call that eventually replaces you.

I have been so blessed in the friendship department. If there is one thing I am eternally grateful for every single day, it's that I have had and still have the best friends ever.

When you have those 'truest friends' you can have your little punch-ups and still be absolutely fine with one another. You can have fights or arguments with true friends – there's nothing like a healthy debate. It's like having fights as brothers and sisters: you just get over that shit real quick because your love is so pure.

The friend you do fall out with, and even though you say sorry you can't come back from that ... they're no true friend. If you are genuinely sorry and willing to do whatever you can to keep that friendship alive – within reason, of course – but they're going to make you do insane things for their ego, well, come on, don't play the fool now: that's not true friendship anyway.

True friends will always forgive you no matter what. They will forgive and understand if you're acting strangely because you are going through a hard time or if you have done the wrong thing or something stupid.

Like I said, if you didn't find your soul sisters as a youngster, they are still comin', girls and boys! Don't give up on that because there are so many magical souls out there.

I think we spend a lot of time focusing on the bad people, but if we sit down every day and list all the things we are grateful for and all the people we are grateful for, we realise how magical the world is and how magical people can be.

CHAPTER 12

Tom and Yvie

I tend to find that when I am down in the dumps I constantly think of myself. I compare myself to others and I am forever looking at ways I can better myself physically, emotionally or spiritually. I am at my happiest when I am the least of my worries and all I think of are ways in which I can help other people or get involved in causes that make my heart sing.

One of my greatest achievements to date was living with Tom Hancock.

Tom is a now 38-year-old man with Down syndrome and type 1 diabetes.

I moved in with Tom in 2013 when I was just a 23-year-old lass, only two years fresh in Sydney. I spent those first two years either interning my butt off for free or working those long production hours during the week (as I mentioned earlier in this book), and by the weekend I was Kings Cross's number one fan.

I would hit up those R'n'B clubs with my best friend, Sarah, and my cousin Carly like I had never heard music before. We would legit crump until six in the morning most weekends. Ahhh, those were the days.

I feel that is what you gotta do when you first move to Sydney. I was so lucky because none of those lock-out laws had come to town yet and Kings Cross was the place to be. Now it is just full of 24-hour-access gyms and kebab shops. What a goddamn contradiction, number one, and number two: how freakin' boring! Bring back the 24-hour clubs and, yeah, keep the kebab shops, I'm okay with that.

But back to the story …

One day, out of the blue, just like when Harry met Sally (but nothing like that at all), Angie met Yvie.

How did we meet, I hear you ask? Well, I will put the Tom story aside for a moment and tell you the tale. It goes a little something like this …

Twenty-one-year-old Angie was living her best unstable but incredibly fun life in Queens Park, in the eastern suburbs. New to Sydney, she was working them long hours as an intern on set for television commercials, post-production coordinating for some of Australia's most iconic documentaries, working as a fashion styling assistant, transcribing … oh, the list can go on and on.

In short: Angie was doing exactly what she wanted to do when she had the idea to move to Sydney after graduating from her degree in Brisbane.

There was just one thing missing ... she was not getting paid to work these dream jobs. You've got to start from the damn bottom in this film/television production industry, you'd best believe that.

So Angie worked as a nanny during the week when she wasn't interning and on the weekends she figured, 'Hey, why not do a bit of promotional work? I'm young, I'm freshly single, I don't know many people in Sydney yet, so why not get into some promo to earn some extra squirrels and make some new mates?'

Thinking she would get a job in the clubs or handing out some lame drink for free at the train stations (and I did the second one: my drink-handing-out skills are on fleek), oh, how wrong she was, indeedy doo.

Amongst the drink handouts and a few other promotional gigs that must have been so incredibly insignificant as she simply cannot remember any of them in detail, there was the Miranda Westfield Christmas promotion.

Wait, it gets better.

Angie had to get through the orientation meeting first. Sitting in the meeting room with other struggling wannabe creatives like herself, she felt all right about the current set-up.

The turnout was to be expected. Then in walks this beautifully loud and inappropriate woman, a fair bit older than the rest of the infants that filled the room, but by no means would you have been able to guess her age. No-sirree-Bob.

The lady was late and slightly flustered but totally brushed it off with them dazzling pearly whites and the ability to laugh at herself. This was Angie's kind of girl.

Angie would find out down the track, when the first shift started, that she would be an elf. A friggin' Christmas elf who would hand out free samples of food made by the surrounding shops. And that beautifully loud woman, Yvie – Yvie was Mrs Claus, ladies and gentlemen. How good is that?

So Yvie and I met while we were both in need of some dirty quick cash and I was the elf to her Mrs Claus.

It is safe to say the rest is history.

Yvie made me laugh constantly with her incredibly inappropriate sense of humour transmitted over a microphone while she was supposed to be wishing everyone a Merry Christmas and selling the shit out of the food. Instead she would make up lyrics to traditional Christmas songs and proclaim on her microphone, 'I am Mrs Claus, and I am beautiful.'

Whoever decided to give that woman a microphone in a shopping centre is both genius and absolutely insane. But my god ... did we laugh.

The laughter and the inappropriateness were the start of this stronger-than-strong friendship. Don't let anyone tell you that age should be a concern with any relationship, because age is certainly just a number. Yvie is seventeen years my senior and she neither looks or acts like it.

Now let's do a 360 back to where this story was going.

Thanks to Yvie Justice Jones, I met Tommy. When I first met Yvie she lived in Potts Point with her two beautiful dogs, Oscar and Leo. I would visit her and we would paint the town red and have YouTube viewing parties while smashing copious amounts of wine.

Then Yvie moved out to the inner west. If you are a Sydney person reading this book, you will know that in the Sydney world that is like moving to a different country. People from the eastern suburbs joke that they need their passport to cross the bridge to the inner west. Having lived in both the east of Sydney and the inner west, I can safely say that ... inner west is the best, inner west is where it's at!

So Yvie moved inner west to a little suburb called Stanmore, and Stanmore was where Mr Thomas Hancock lived.

Tom's set-up is amazing. The way it works is that Tom has two housemates who live in his home that his parents bought for him at the ripe old age of twenty-one to help him integrate into the community and allow him to live his very best life. The two people who live with Tom assist him with everyday living and monitoring his diabetes, and in return for their care and time they live in the house free of charge.

Yvie and Tom were living with another man at the time and then, when he moved out of the house, Yvie started working her magic. Having me over for dinners every week, getting me to look after her baby boys while she went out.

Home girl was totally buttering me up to see how I was with Tom and the dogs. She seduced me with food, dogs and an amazing speech about how much money I would save if I moved in with her and Tom.

After some serious consideration I eventually said yes. It was a big decision to make. I was living with my amazing cousin Carly at the time and I had a beautiful little home in Queens Park for quite cheap rent considering the location, which is also unheard of in Sydney.

Mostly though I was worried about the responsibility of looking after Tom. I wasn't sure if I would be the best person for him, as I had no idea about diabetes and how serious it was, nor did I know how to care for a man with Down syndrome.

But I loved Tom so much – he had become my friend over these visits – and I adored the dogs and Yvie, and living there would mean I could put my drink handout days to bed and really start focusing on more paid gigs in the industry. So I said yes!

Living with Tom and taking care of him was like a partnership. I felt as if I was taking on a massive responsibility at quite a young age. With saying that, I wouldn't have had it any other way. Tom taught me so much and has given me that many lol moments in my life that I could never have found anywhere else!

I witnessed some hypoglycaemic attacks from Tommy during my stay. They would frighten the absolute living daylights out of me. A grown man not knowing who you are or where he is, watching his body go into shutdown mode and having to force-feed him like a baby could be terrifying. As time went on I got more comfortable with and confident about handling these attacks, and they became less frequent too, which was a bonus.

In 2014 I made a documentary called *Tom's Plan* that demonstrated how Tom's living arrangements worked and all the joy they brought me (if you have the time you should totally check it out).

Yvie and I would take Tom out for dinners like a little family or we would take turns at staying home and going out, as we also had our separate work and social lives too.

My friends would come over and we would have barbecues at the Stanmore house, and Tom would put on shows. We were always entertaining and Tom was always involved.

People would often stare at Tom and me when we were out together, or they would ask questions. Which I loved. Some people could be ignorant but others wanted to learn. It is always best to educate not hate.

I enjoyed seeing the looks on their faces when they found out that Tom was not my brother or a family member and that he was my housemate and one of my best friends. I remember one person asked me why would someone so young, who could be out with boys and partying with friends, want to sit at a pub with someone like Tom?

I would always answer people's questions with another question – in that case, and for other similar questions, I said, 'Well, why not?'

They would kind of look at me, all confused. Some would get it and others just didn't.

I think if you are a naturally caring and compassionate person, there is no question as to why a person would hang out with someone who not only relies on your assistance but loves you to pieces.

Tom always lives in the moment. He does not hold grudges. He can chuck the biggest tantrums and can be a little bit spoilt from time to time, but I have friends who are completely able-bodied who carry on more than Tom and his mates do. And no one ever asks me why I hang out with them.

So my answer was always: 'Why not?'

Why not spend nearly every day laughing and giving back to a human being who just wants to live his best damn life like the rest of us?

I lived at Tom's house for three and a half years. Some days were bloody hard and other days were pure bliss.

Tom is still very much involved in my life. My friends know him, my family knows him. He comes and stays on the Sunshine Coast for holidays with me and visits my family. We have been to Bali together twice; we even travelled all the way to the UK together. Now, *that* was an interesting 24-plus-hours flight. Injecting a 30-something-year-old man with his insulin needles on a plane and force-feeding him every two hours so he didn't go into a massive hypoglycaemic attack on one of those long flights. But it was worth it to have him on the trip. Lots of things can seem like they're too hard, but when you think about why you're doing them – and what they bring to your life – they're not hard at all.

•

Watching TV for a living is a pretty sweet gig ... but do you know what is even sweeter? Looking after people with a disability.

After I moved out of Tom's home to travel and live between London and Sydney, I missed living with him. So I got my qualifications to become a support worker. I was now officially getting paid to hang out with one of my best friends. How good!

I had a couple of other clients too. These clients were Tom's best friends. So every Tuesday we would go to drama class (my god, was that one of the best drama classes I have seen in a long time) then we would go about the inner west trying out new pubs and restaurants, or we would go to the movies or do trivia.

It wasn't always fun and games, though – Tom and his friends can certainly put on a big ol' drama performance outside of drama class too. There was plenty of verbal punch-up shared between mates. I guess like any friendship, really. Though maybe more like a friendship on steroids.

The emotions they feel are so pure and so real and they have no problems in expressing them. I found that so magical and truthful: to be able to express yourself completely and to not give a flying rat's ass about what anyone else thinks about you or the situation you are in.

I think we can all learn a little something from Tom and his friends. We can learn to live in the moment and express ourselves. Leave all this passive–aggressive bullshit at the door and really express how we feel, when we feel it. How much sense does that make?

We tend to overcomplicate most things by being so polite and not saying how we feel but then saying it to every Tom, Dick and Harry behind the back of the actual person we are angry at. Why do we do this? It is infuriating.

I do it too sometimes and then I think, well, that was just pointless. I could've nipped that right in the bud when it happened by saying, 'Hey, now, I'm not overly into this' or 'This doesn't sit well with me – can we maybe not do this now or this way?'

I could sit here forever and list all the things I have learnt from living with Tom, but there is one thing that stands out the most and that is that I'm a much better person for knowing him. Tom was and still is my family.

CHAPTER 13

Dogs

I am pretty damn blessed to have shared those years living with Tom and my soul sister Yvie. Not only did we care for Tom, we also rescued, fostered and rehomed hundreds of dogs during my time there.

That house was seriously Central Station, but for all the hounds, not humans. And that gives me the chance to talk about 'Foster Problems'. (Foster Problems – or FP – is kind of like 'White People Problems' or 'First World Problems', but is obviously for foster parents.)

The reason I feel strongly about including this is, well, because (a) FP was always happening to us, and (b) people would often ask how we did it. How did we say goodbye to so many of the dogs who would come in and out of our lives?

Most of the time we answered positively, by saying that it's just what we had to do and we were happy that we could make a difference in the lives of the dog and the people who were looking for their perfect furry soul mate. But some days I felt bloody sorry for myself and I want to admit that, yes, sometimes it could be very hard!

There were so many dogs that I wanted to have stay with me forever, but they would either have to go back to their owners who got out of hospital or jail, or they had to move on to their next home, as our home was just the stop-off.

There was more than one dog who stole my heart, but there was one in particular I thought could stay with me forever. I would get into these negative thought patterns and think the owner didn't deserve to have her back, and that we'd created a special bond.

I would say to the universe, 'If she is meant to be mine, then please let this owner surrender her and then I know she's meant to be with me forever.'

Her name was Tinee and she was my princess in fur.

I would carry her around to work and take her to dinner. She would sleep with me every night. I would introduce her to friends and the children I was looking after at the time as if she was my very own. Everyone who met her just adored her.

Tinee Girl really felt like mine, my little pocket rocket. But she was not mine and I needed to understand that, at that point in time, this particular dog was not mine. I was just her little helper and she was my little helper through our rough patches, while her owner sorted himself out, and while I needed some extra loving without even realising it.

I didn't just do her a favour by looking after her: she did me a massive favour too. I got to love something unconditionally! To have a best friend, and both keep each other safe and happy.

I also came to the conclusion that maybe her owner needed her more than I did, and as much as I wanted to be selfish and say I needed her too, that was not what the universe had in store.

I knew there were plenty of other little soul mates just waiting for Yvie and me to rescue them, and for them to rescue us for however long they were in our lives.

Our original gangsters, as I like to call them, were Charlie Bear – who is now with Yvie's dad – and our big old hot messes Stella and Mardi Ma. We got Stells Bells and Mardi Ma roughly around the same time, which was about when we started filming the first season of *Gogglebox*. I guess these two are the ones to thank for our fostering addiction.

We got the girls through Paws and Recover, a registered not-for-profit organisation which is establishing an infrastructure of volunteers to support people by sharing the care of their pets during a health crisis or difficult time.

Stella is a gorgeous staffy cross. We refer to Stella as a foster fail because she ain't going nowhere. Her forever home is right here with us.

Stella had the most horrendous start to life. This is what was written when Stella was first found by RSPCA and picked up by Paws and Recover:

Picked up this little girl today. Terrible truth is she has been sexually abused, she is timid and withdrawn (but not a biter). Giving her time to heal and learn that the world can be fun. She will be looking for a loving home in the near future.

After we found out what had happened to Stella in her earlier stages of life, we helped rehabilitate her into the cheeky, happy little girl she is today.

Mardi Ma, a big beautiful dingo cross kelpie, had to leave us after an entire year to go back to her very-much-missed mumma, who got out of jail.

Handing Mardi over was one of the hardest things I had to do. She protected me when I felt I needed protection the most.

But we felt so blessed to have had the time with her and return her to her best friend. We thought we were doing the right thing at the time, giving her back to her owner, because Mardi was all that this lady had.

We found out a year or so later that Mardi Ma had died.

We were told she died of a heart attack. There were also rumours that she had been killed by people who her owner owed money to. But we like to imagine that Mardi died peacefully in her sleep and that we did the right thing by giving her back to her owner.

This lady had nothing else and was fresh out of jail, living in a halfway home. Mardi and her spent eleven years together before Mardi was taken from her and this lady had no idea where Mardi was going when she was thrown into jail. Mardi was due to be put down when Paws and Recover intervened and took her on, promising her owner we would give her back.

Her owner even got to watch Mardi on the couch, on *Gogglebox*, from jail. She told us that it made her so happy to see Mardi in such good hands.

We miss you, our queen, and we know you are in a much better place.

You do always think 'what if?', though, don't you? It is hard not to. What if we didn't give Mardi Ma back to her owner like we had promised? Would she still be alive? But we try not to think about it and hope that her last year was pure happiness with her owner who we could see loved her so much.

They had a rough life together living on the streets but they always had each other, and to us that was beautiful.

Let me tell you a little bit about the magic that is Paws and Recover. Paws and Recover is run by a fantastic woman with a heart bigger than Australia! Her name is Jacki and she is a bloody legend. Not only does Jacki work full time, she's set up this organisation out of her own home.

Jacki can have up to ten dogs at a time. If you think you saw a lot of pooches on our couch back in the *Gogglebox* days, you ain't seen nuttin!

We would help Jacki out by reposting her updates from the Paws and Recover Facebook page to our contacts so that more people would be able to join her list of volunteers, whether it was for fostering for a few days (or weeks or months, depending on availability, there is never any pressure), dog walking, transporting dogs to homes or taking them to vet appointments and so on.

Of course, we also took dogs under our wings and we would have them from as little as a few days to as long as a year.

If a pooch was available for adoption, we would try to help find their forever home by asking people at the park or people we knew. There's a thorough check that goes on to make sure it's the right loving family and home for each dog, but we always kept a lookout for the potential perfect home. You just never know who's out there!

Just like anything, fostering dogs has its ups and its downs. What always got us through was knowing that we would much rather have had the dogs in our lives than to never have had them at all.

You can't have light without darkness, happiness without understanding sadness, and so on and so forth.

I would rather have had my baby dogs even for a short period than to not have had them all up in my grill for that time.

And, no, the amount of dog shit I have stepped on in my own home still has not turned me off wanting bulk dogs.

For the love of god, people, please, if you only get one thing out of this nonstop dribble that I am sharing with you, it should be this: #adoptdontshop! I ain't here to hate, I'm here to educate.

If there are two things I know, they are: (a) I know nothing at all, (b) except how important it is to adopt and not shop for your pooch.

Why should you adopt and not shop? Because when you adopt, you are saving two lives.

The first life you save is the life of the pet you adopt – and each adoption creates space in a shelter or rescue home for another animal to be rescued. So that's two lives saved.

Each year millions of adoptable dogs and cats are put down simply because too many pets are dropped off at shelters; sometimes it's just because the owner can no longer look after the pet, not because the animal is a menace.

Some people hold on to this absolutely untrue idea that every dog that is at a shelter or rescue home must have some serious issues. NOT TRUE.

Some of the busiest times of the year for rescue shelters are after Christmas and Valentine's Day. Why? Because people buy their partners a cute little poochie woochie as a gift and after a solid few weeks of real life – when it is an absolute shitting machine that tears up all your fave things – they think, *Yeah nah not for me*, and they pop the pooch online or send it to their local shelter.

It is totally fine if puppies are not for you or the fam. Puppies are bloody hard work. This is another fabulous reason as to why you should adopt: you don't have to commit to a puppy! You can get a four-year-old that is totally toilet trained, or an eight-year-old who just loves to lie around with you and be your best friend.

You know what you are getting when you adopt a dog. When you buy a puppy from a puppy mill, you have no idea what you are in for. Not to mention that you probably have no idea what that poor mother dog has been through.

I have heard some horrifying stories about what they do to those poor dogs in puppy mills or puppy farms. I won't go down that path but do yourself a favour and do a little Google search when you have the chance. Or follow the amazing story that is behind Oscar's Law and the sensational work they do. I get insane goosebumps just thinking about it.

Also remember this: for about 90 per cent of the pets that come into pounds or shelters, something has happened in their little lives that has put them there. It generally has nothing to do with the pet.

Plus, I have never met a bad dog that was just born bad. Something has to happen to them for them to react or act badly and it is generally caused by something that starts with H and ends with N. Just sayin'.

So if you are thinking about adding a pooch to your fam, then by all means get amongst it. Dog truly is a human's best friend.

Just remember to #adoptdontshop and save a little life.

CHAPTER 14

Home

I think that home is where you are happy. Sounds very simple, doesn't it? And it very well can be.

The reason why I think this is because I have lived in so many different houses, in so many different areas, and I wasn't happy in the majority of them.

I have to say that my all-time safe zone is my family home on the Sunshine Coast. There I can be a little grot; I can just lie in bed all day and I don't feel judged.

Most of my memories are from there; a lot of my bits and pieces are there – though they never used to be there and I was fine without them because I was happy.

I know that I can always come back to this safe place when I am gallivanting between lifestyles. That's where my family is so that is probably the main reason why it feels like home to me.

For the last couple of years I have been house sitting and pet sitting across Sydney while also living in England. So it's safe to say I had many homes. I was living out of a suitcase for pretty much two freakin' years. Heck, I still *am* living out of a suitcase most of the time.

I had stuff in storage, or in my car; I was going to a new house every week, getting new animals to look after every week. It was so exhausting.

I was even staying with friends and sleeping on their couches when there were no house sits lined up.

It got to the point that I was so incredibly run-down that I managed to get shingles while I was working full time as a nanny, filming for *Gogglebox*, moving every few days trying to save all the money I could to get myself back to the UK where I still bloody lived on struggle street most of the time.

I had all these sometimes-beautiful places that offered me a roof over my head, but by no means did they feel like home.

That's because I wasn't happy.

But then there was this one time when I lived in the African jungle, in nature, right under them sweet, sweet stars. I was sleeping in the most uncomfortable beds, either freezing cold or boiling hot. I was so hot and sweaty that my sleeping bag was soaking wet from detoxing and starving out of my damn mind. But that was one of the happiest times of my life.

That little, basic and sometimes frightening set-up in the jungle felt like home to me.

Why? Because I was so happy with who I was and how I was feeling around the crazy beautiful people I was with.

When I was staying in some of the most beautiful houses in the northern beaches and the eastern suburbs of Sydney, nannying in mansions in Sussex in England and Spain and Greece, in the most comfortable beds, I wasn't happy. That didn't feel like home to me. I didn't feel safe. I didn't feel comfortable. I was always kind of on edge.

So now I thoroughly believe that home is where you are happy. Home is where your heart lies. If you're happy with a little knapsack in the jungle, in a tent on the beach, well, then, that's your home. Home is where you feel that happiness in your heart.

Maybe home to you could mean the people you're with. You could be sleeping on a rock but you're with your soul mates, and that may feel like home to you.

Or if you have all your favourite bits and pieces around you but you're out in a paddock, that could be your version of home. As long as you are happy.

I now realise that I don't need much at all. I am actually quite the simpleton.

The jungle made me realise this. Staying in those fancy houses felt more like a chore. Staying out in Mother Nature – the ultimate MILF – breathing in the smoky air of the leftover fire from the night before and going to the toilet four times a night because I was so dehydrated I drank my body weight in water during the day, going to the toilet in a long and short drop where snakes could crawl right up ya noonka ... that just felt like my home.

When I left that place I thought, *Nooooooo, I can't go back to normal living. This is my home now!* It was the best feeling in the world to be there and I didn't want to leave it.

Now I'm back in Australia and back at my family home again, I do feel very blessed, but it is slightly overwhelming, of course. I am used to doing whatever the hell I want. I'm out all day, I'm out all night. Sometimes I don't even come home 'cause Imma grown-ass woman.

When you're back at the 'rents you do need to let them know if you're alive – which is understandable, of course, but it's hard to come to terms with when you're so used to being a gypsy.

It's actually quite funny that I am so content in my family home. It's like Central Station up in there, so hectic with all of us kids coming in and out and everyone working different hours, and yet I still feel so comfortable there.

I know a lot of people who couldn't think of anything worse than living back home with their parents and brothers and sisters, but I feel safest there even though they drive me nuts.

So I definitely think home is where you're happy and it's not necessarily having the fanciest set-up. It's just where your little heart feels at ease and at peace.

There's nothing better than, after a huge-ass day, being in your comfort zone. I live my life out of the comfort zone. I have done so since I finished school. Even though I have crazy anxiety, I get off on just pushing myself to the limit – which isn't the greatest habit, I know, but I do expect so much from myself.

I would never let my anxiety stop me from doing things. I have never stayed in a comfort zone just because my anxiety might be on fire and it would be better if I stayed home and did what my anxiety wants me to do. I can't let it win.

I could be filming for something, or doing a radio interview, or going out west to pick up a dog whose owner has neglected it. I am generally doing something out of the ordinary because I believe that's what life is all about.

It's okay to embrace the uncertainty in your life. Doesn't make you an extremist.

I am also a massive simpleton too. Even though I love to live my life out of the stock-standard box, I also love to come home and do sweet FA. Just being in my bed, being able to do whatever the hell I want, with whoever the hell I want, or mainly by my lonesome.

So in conclusion to this sensational little rant: home is where the heart is, my sweet thangs. Find what your heart loves and know that there is your home. No judgement.

CHAPTER 15

Single Status

I've never understood why people don't like being single. I mean, I get it if you're older and you've done a solid amount of YOU time and you know what you want and it's been a long time since you've had some sweet tender loving from a partner – but all these young women that are like twenty-five say, 'Ohh, I've been single for so long [like five years]! I just really want to find someone! I'm so sick of being single.'

To that I say: 'Girl! One day there's a solid chance you will get married and have kids if you see fit, and then you're kind of stuck with that fella, the father of your kids, for a long-ass time. So while you have no commitments, and absolute freedom to do whatever the hell you want (within reason, of course), why not get amongst it? There's an entire world out there to explore and, believe you me, it's bloody beautiful.'

Single time is your time to get to know yourself, explore yourself, travel, study, date all the wrong guys (or girls) so you know who the right person is when they come knocking on your door.

If only it was that easy! Oh, how good – imagine if it *was* that easy? Imagine if one day, when it's the right time, the right fella just comes and literally knocks on your door and is like, 'Hey, I'm ready too, let's do this.'

Well, it kind of *is* like that, if you really think about it. The universe, if we let it, always sends us what we need at the right time.

Because we are so impatient we just go and date every Tom, Dick and Harry because we are 'sick of being single'. I mean, don't get me wrong – I understand that it's not as easy and simple as a guy comes a-knockin' on your front door. But he (or she) does eventually come if you trust and allow the universe to do its thing.

It would be so nice if we could all just flow a little more. Like, when the shit hits the fan maybe we don't lose our minds and we just accept that it's so shit but we're meant to go through this shit right now. We don't know why, but we're sure it will teach us something down the track and lead us to where we are supposed to be.

Just sit in the shit, feel it to heal it, don't make it more shit by asking forty-four million questions and saying, '*Why me?*'

Why you? Why *everybody*?

We all go through ups and downs, some more heavily than others. That's life.

Life is scary and hard, but sometimes it's so magical and beautiful. All part of the flow.

Nothing ever stays the same, so we must grow and flow with it.

There's a great saying: 'Never get attached to moments good or bad – nothing lasts forever.' It's kind of sad but it's true. The quicker we realise that nothing does stay the same and we're forever changing and growing, the happier we will be.

All we have is right now, my sweet thangs. The past is merely a memory and the future is out of our control. So accept the now.

How beautiful and simple. I wish it were that easy! All in good practice: it's like riding a bike. Everything takes time and patience and persistence.

So back to the single situation … I've been on some fabulous dates in my time. I peaked super young in the boyfriend and good dates department, but that's okay because since then I've had a solid seven to eight years to date myself.

Myself and I haven't always had the best of times, though, don't get me wrong. We have had some rubbish dates together. Absolutely dreadful breakups. I've given myself a lifelong eating disorder, drunk myself into spewing sprees, and pushed myself to the limit physically and mentally over the years.

I have been a real asshole to myself at times. I have acknowledged this and have accepted it, and all I do now is move forward and love myself a little more every day.

Working on ourselves is the fun part. We should never get sick of bettering ourselves – how magical that we have the opportunity to do so.

Now this girl who has been single for such a long time, and has been so frightened to be vulnerable around a partner, has put herself into the ultimate dating challenge. The time is right – I *know* it is. Whatever happens, I am ready for this experience. But if I hadn't taken all that time to be on my own, and get to know myself better, I know I wouldn't be able to have the relationship I want.

I will not lose myself inside a relationship – I will *be* myself, with the best possible plus one.

CHAPTER 16

Loving Your Imperfections

I'm sure with all of us there are parts of our personality or body that we just can't seem to love.

I have super-weird knees, for example. They're so fugly. One has a massive scar on it and the other is so swollen from a virus that attacked my knee at the ripe young age of sixteen, swelled it up like a boss and then it seemed to never go back to normal.

But then I think without that scar or swollen knee, would I be the me I am now? The me who has stories about why these knees are so ratchet?

What's a life without our tales? Imagine being so perfect you had no real stories to share because everything was so boringly in proportion.

Yes, I have suffered terribly from pain with the left knee that swells up every time I stand on it for too long or even try to be a lady and wear high-heeled shoes, and the search for answers has been exhausting and expensive.

But without it, would I be the girl I am today?

Without the scar on my right knee I would never have the story of how my aunty and uncle took me to a water park and I was running around the pool area (see, this is the reason why they say don't run on slippery surfaces, people) and I went ass over tits in what felt like slow-mo and cracked my jaw out of place and completely smashed my knee open.

I went back to my Poppy and Nan's place where I spent a lot of my childhood, and my Poppy Ted refused to send me to the hospital because he didn't want them to scar my beautiful knees (his words – not mine). I was his princess and he didn't want no battle wounds on my little fresh legs.

So we kicked it old school and he kept me up with him on the couch and dressed it himself, putting Betadine on it every few hours to clean the infection. It stung so hardcore I screamed every time he put it on.

It sounds ghastly but every time I look at the scar I end up getting teary because Poppy was no doctor, let's face it, but I think of him. It's my little memory of how much he loved me and wanted to care for me himself and thought I was the best thing since sliced bread.

Now I look at it and I can't imagine that scar not being on my weird alien-looking knees.

Another thing that makes me *me* which I still find hard to love is my little sweaty mittens. I'm not talking nervous sweat that can be brushed off because it's quite cute and endearing. I'm talking don't-go-chasing-waterfalls sweaty. As in, my party trick is legit 'making it rain'.

But wait, there's more: it's not just my hands. It's also my little kangaroo feet. They sweat like crazy too.

I can self-deprecate the shit out of myself but I wouldn't be me without these sweat machines. Even though they drive me nuts and I sometimes get so embarrassed about how moist (yes, I just used the word *moist*) my hands get, and how many times I have been freezing cold because I have wiped these out-of-control sweaty pricks on my beautiful clothes so that my clothing is soaking wet.

Seriously, though, if you have hyperhidrosis and it bothers you – as it can cause extreme anxiety – there are a lot of remedies you can look in to, which I am happy to share with you. So hit me up if you're a sweat queen or king like me and need some advice.

I can fill you in on one remedy (otherwise we would be here for days) and that's ol' faithful Botox in your hands. Hurts like a bitch and takes a while to kick in and is not cheap at all, but my god it's worth a shot (love a good pun). And, again, what another tale to tell.

Ahhhh, ain't life grand.

I have it all, people: I've suffered from irritable bowel syndrome, acne and acne scarring, being one of the sweatiest people in Australia (I just gave myself that title), anxious as all hell, endometriosis, coeliac disease, swollen and scarred knees, spells of chronic depression where I feel like I won't see the light of day again, lost the love of my life – but without these things I wouldn't be where I am and who I am.

And you know what, I'm sure I could have saved thousands on medical bills and not been so mortified with embarrassment on many occasions, but I wouldn't have all these tales and what's life without experiences and being able to share and connect?

Love the weird shit you've got because none of us are perfect.

If you think what you see on Instagram or any form of social media is perfect ... I'm sorry, you are wrong. Don't be too envious because I am sure half of those people who look perfect on socials wish they had some of the shit that you have.

CHAPTER 17

Love Your Body Well

I wasn't very nice to myself throughout my mid to late teens and into my mid-twenties. As you do when you're going through this thing we call life. We live and we learn, but I did a whole lot of living for a while.

Sometimes as humans we get stuck in a rut or a routine and we don't realise how unhealthy it is, but as you get older you work out how damn important it is to look after yourself – because it's only when you're older that you start feeling everything you have done to yourself.

When I was younger I thought I could numb my problems with a big ol' Maccas cheese burger, drinking all night and sleeping all day. But if you are anything like me you hit your mid-twenties and your body's like, *Ahhhhhh yeah, remember that you treated me like shit for about a solid two or so years? Well, payback's a bitch.*

So I wasn't very kind to myself. I look back now and I think this came down to many reasons, one being I wasn't overly educated about my body: on how much damage I was doing to my body and not understanding my emotions, and how important it is to know 'you are what you eat' and your body is listening to every little thought you think – and often our thoughts can be pretty hardcore too.

When I was fourteen I went to a naturopath for my acne which I had started getting at about eleven years old. I got to high school and I had braces, and I was still rocking some mean-ass piggytails, and then I got rid of those and started to get a bit more attention from the fellas because I did look quite mature for my age: I was blonde and was actually classified tall, but funnily enough I have stayed the same height since I was about twelve and my breasts have stayed the same too. So, yeah, cheers for that, universe – I'm still rockin' a twelve-year-old girl's body. Just with a little bit more fat – woooo!

So I went to a naturopath to find out what I was doing wrong with my skin and why my skin was so wild.

The naturopath said, and I remember this as clear as day: 'You are what you eat.' Which is true to some degree, but it really isn't the best thing to tell a very sensitive and susceptible teenage gal.

I believe I needed to be way more educated on that saying before I jumped right on board and took her word as bible.

I was only young; that was such a full-on thing to hear, because then I instantly thought, *Great: now I can't eat anything except lettuce leaves.*

I didn't know what was good for me, to fuel my body, mind and soul, to make me the very best teenage version of Angie I could be.

I don't believe we were overly educated on those things at school. Schools were still selling bulk meat pies and pizza rounders, which were way too tempting for growing and hormonal teenage boys and girls. I know that nowadays, and just as I was leaving school the whole health kick came to town and more healthier options became available, which is great.

But for me, at that time, I thought I had to give up everything and just live off salad. Being incredibly hormonal, though, you want to smash bulk treats during that time of month – ladies, can I get an amen? We can crave the most insane things during that time of the month. Mine are generally like condiments on top of things, salty stuff like chips, and even though I am lactose-intolerant I crave the hell out of bulk cheeses.

It's so weird: I don't eat dairy but I crave cheese. And being young I would just listen to those cravings and smash that. I went from eating salads all the time and being way too OTT with what I was eating, to then getting my period and not being able to control these cravings, and smashing all these foods I wasn't supposed to eat.

This is where it gets a bit sad, friends – just a heads-up.

I would be so mortified, like I had committed some kind of crime eating these foods. I would beat myself up so much that my parents had spent so much money on sending me to this naturopath, which wasn't overly heard of back in the early 2000s – it was quite a new and alternative route to go down and expensive as all hell.

So when I did binge I would just throw it all up. Thinking that it wouldn't affect my skin if I got rid of it.

From there it turned into an addiction. I was well and truly obsessed. I went from only throwing up junk food to then throwing up sandwiches and then eventually I was throwing up my dinner every night.

Things weren't great at home back then; there wasn't a lot of love shown between my mum and dad. When I was a teenager my dad often wouldn't talk to me and I never felt like I was doing anything right, always getting into trouble.

That feeling of everything being out of my control.

The only control I had in my life was what I put in my mouth. I could control everything that went into my body, and when I lost that control and put something bad into my body, I then had the control to get it out of my body.

So I kept throwing up my food.

It almost became an escape for me. If I hadn't done it, I would think about doing it, so it was just better I got it over and done with.

I liked the feeling of it too – the release of the food coming out. I was just so addicted.

Plus, I didn't know any better: I started doing it when I was fourteen, so by the time I was in my early twenties I almost forgot what it was like to not do it.

Then, when I was sixteen, I went on Roaccutane, and Roaccutane made me a bloody crazy person, because ... well, it just does. Little side note for y'all: don't go on Roaccutane until you are well and truly out of puberty. Take my word.

This medicine brought out all the bad stuff in my skin, so I was rocking these mean-ass welty pimples. They were bloody and horrible and looked like cysts.

Of course, you're not supposed to pop them, and I would because I didn't want to go to school looking like that because teenagers are mean and everyone would just stare at me and call me pizza face, so I would pop them. And that, kids, is how you end up with acne scars.

So, yes, it's safe to say I wasn't very kind to myself during my younger years.

Living with an eating disorder, especially in high school, and being able to hide it – I actually did a pretty solid job of this. I think everyone noticed I was getting really skinny but I think they mainly thought it was because I didn't eat much due to my new-found skin obsession. I don't think people knew the degree of what was actually going on and how much I was throwing up and how much this obsession dictated my life.

I remember stopping, or at least cutting back a whole lot for a while, when I got this amazing boyfriend who was quite a bit older than me. He didn't drink, he didn't party, he was super chilled and smart and funny. We would go out and eat healthier foods, always be at the beach, and just go and do more active stuff. And I got to escape high school. I got to feel that love and I didn't feel the need to treat myself badly anymore – he almost distracted me from what I didn't like in my life.

I was so swept up in him and me, and being the best I could be at school. He motivated and inspired me. Mainly because he thought I was the bee's knees and butter wouldn't melt, and I thought the exact same thing about him.

I was very lucky to have experienced a soul mate at such a young age. We don't talk anymore, but if he ever sees this I hope he knows how much he meant to me and to my family. Cheers, CT.

Then, obviously, with leaving school and getting out into the real world and breaking up with my boyfriend who was such a big part of that time of my life, everything felt out of control again.

And what did I do when I felt out of control? You guessed it, I spewed. Whenever I would eat too much food, I would throw it up.

It wasn't even about my skin anymore. I also got addicted to being skinny and, as I mentioned, I was mainly addicted to the control.

I got better as I got older when I started to understand my body and my mental health more, but it never goes away. It's like any addiction. Even when you are an alcoholic and give up the booze, you're still a recovering alcoholic for the rest of your life. You're fighting that battle every day.

So even though I am so much more mindful of this illness and what my body wants and needs, I slip up from time to time with treats – I'm only human. Then the old guilt creeps in, that little negative voice that pops into my head and says, 'Yuck, you're fat! People are looking at what you are eating, people think you are a pig.' Now, though, if I eat too much food or the wrong foods, there's that strong Angie voice that's like, 'Girl, listen to your body, if it's hungry eat what you want – you can always work it out later. Go to the gym, you will go back to your normal routine the next day.'

I went from 48 kilos to gaining a lot of weight in my mid-twenties because I went on a different anti-anxiety medication, and I was coeliac but still smashing gluten, so I was swollen as all hell and my mental health was off the Richter.

Going to 60 kilos, I was mortified. I got off the anti-anxiety meds, mainly because they weren't working for me, not because I gained some extra cushion – but obviously that played a huge part in my anxiety. The anti-anxiety meds just didn't sit well with me anymore, and the more I learnt about mental health the more I wanted to do it all natural.

I gave up gluten for good, said 'Bye Felicia' to the white wine a.k.a. lady petrol a.k.a. Argie juice. (Argie Bargie was my alter ego name created by my soul sister Yvie Jones – we can touch on this alter ego later, or not, because she was a real mole, Argie, and I don't really want to even give her any air time. She can stay in the past with the lady petrol and gluten where they all belong.)

So I stopped smashing burgers and white wine. I mean, come on, I still love me a drink, don't get me wrong. I just looked into what was good for my soul, and I started working out.

I can't stay 48 kilos – heck, I don't even think my body would allow it anymore even if I did it the healthy way. It was so sick of being a bag of bones that now every piece of food I eat you can see on my body.

I am still quite small, but I think it's harder for me to lose weight now, especially around my stomach area. This is because I abused my body so much for so long that I gave myself nearly every inflammatory condition one could have. Bingeing and throwing up so much, I believe I gave myself coeliac disease, I gave myself IBS, and now I have endometriosis. My poor little temple was so inflamed.

You are what you eat and what you do to your body, but you need to be educated on what is good for you. You are allowed to treat yourself but then if you worry about what you've eaten, go for a walk. Not just because you want to burn off the food but because it's just so damn good for you and your mental health.

I work hard at the gym sometimes so that I can treat myself, because I deserve it.

Nowadays I more so do what is good for my mind and my body. I don't do it to be skinny or to be in control. Like I said earlier on, that little negative voice is still there but I know how to acknowledge it with ease, not panic and throw up to get rid of its annoying calls. I remember it is merely a thought, and my thoughts don't control me.

Thoughts are just words strung together in sometimes very annoying and damaging sentences. Train yo brain to think with love and light about all things good for that soul of yours.

I know this will always be an addiction of mine, controlling what I do to my body, so I need to be mindful of it and stay on top of it. A great way to do this is by getting into meditation. I see amazing spiritual healers and I have gotten into kinesiology.

I just feel my body and I ask it what it needs. If it does sometimes want to smash a packet of chippies, that's fine. My body is a temple and I need to love it and look after it. I am never going to be that little skinny thang and that's okay because I was so unhealthy and my mental health was at its all-time low, my IBS was off the scale, I was constantly sick with glandular fever or tonsillitis.

I still get run-down when I have done the wrong thing, but now I know how to get myself on track without losing control. My little bod is just so sensitive now because of the damage I caused, and I am making up to it by loving it and looking after it.

Sometimes I rub my little buddha belly and tell it how much I love it, even though I would prefer the little gut part to disappear. But I still love it and I am grateful for everything it has done for me and I am sorry for everything I have put it through.

The most important thing is to keep this fossil healthy, and then the mind stays healthy.

Ever heard the expression 'Trust your gut'? I have made some very questionable decisions in my time. My poor little gut was out of control. If you have ever experienced mental health problems, panic attacks or those long-term anxiety stints where you can't get out of bed, you can't eat, you can't sleep, it's so frightening. You sometimes think you have lost your mind and it isn't coming back – but it does. Your body is just freaking out because its serotonin levels are all wrong.

Once you experience one of those hardcore episodes, you do try to be much kinder to yourself.

Home girl doesn't bounce back like she used to after a hefty night of boozing, and I am okay with that. Because it's happening less frequently these days.

Getting out there and doing stuff that's good for the soul is what gets my juices flowing these days.

You know what, I'm never going to be perfect. Every day I am learning something new about myself, and I am still going to make mistakes because I am a human and I am addicted to that 'I will know for next time' feeling. I just know to be much kinder to my body day to day.

Learn about your body, listen to it, get out of your head and feel where the pain is, and if you do suffer from an eating disorder I highly recommend you speak to someone about it ASAP.

Don't feel ashamed. I know you feel so ashamed when you have an eating disorder but know that you are never alone. There are others out there. And there is help for everyone. You'll always have it – I believe that we are always recovering from an eating disorder – but you just learn that those are obsessive thoughts and put the attention elsewhere, like obsess about being kind to yourself and how you can do that. Kind thoughts instead. It's important to treat yourself and know what your body needs more or less of.

CHAPTER 18

Weight

When I went through the period where I gained a whole lot of weight, it didn't happen all at once. It happened over maybe two years.

If I look back over the photos I notice the difference in my weight gain. So I guess I wasn't really open to scrutiny and I never remember people saying anything or noticing anything from watching me from the first season of *Gogglebox* to season four or five, I think it was. I'd gained quite a bit of weight and I don't ever remember hearing or seeing any online hate, which is totally unheard of because people tend to jump right on that when they say that a woman has gained too much weight or she's changed her face. People are just in there like swimwear. But if there was stuff like that, I didn't see it. Maybe ignorance is bliss.

Maybe I just didn't look. So it didn't affect me at the time. And I don't remember feeling like I had gained that much weight. But I had, and now when I look back at photos of that time I think, *Holy dooley! Sister's face was a bit chunky monkey.* Since I have quite a little frame, people didn't really notice – unless they did and they were just being super polite. And, if so, bless them. That's so kind. Thank you.

I'm sure people said it behind my back because I went from being like unhealthily skinny to being, well, apparently for my height I was in the right weight frame but it wasn't right for me because I was so used to being so underweight. I think some days I got really, really down about it but I don't seem to remember much of that now.

I just look back and think I never want to be that unhealthy again. I was so swollen from consuming gluten because I hadn't been 100 per cent diagnosed coeliac even though I had the disease, and I was smashing those white wines like they were going out of fashion. And I do remember being pretty mentally unwell just because I was eating badly and trying to keep up with everyone else, because there's this stigma around people who have allergies and when you're picky with food some people are actually quite rude and awful about it. They make you feel bad because you don't eat meat or because you're a coeliac or because you can't eat dairy because you were a colicky baby and you will shit your pants. They'll say, 'Why did I invite her for dinner?' It's like, mate, you just worry about you and eat your steak and your chippies and your gravy – I ain't judging and hating on you and I can't-slash-don't-want-to eat any of those things. I'm happy here with my little piece of salmon and my vegetables and my gluten-free chippies, don't you worry about me. You do you, boo.

It always cracks me up when people really get torn up about the fact that I can't eat certain things. I'm just very unsure as to how this is affecting them. I don't know why this is stopping their thought process and filling their mind. Why don't they just enjoy their finer things in life and I'll enjoy mine?

But I guess some people don't understand it. They think I make it up in my head, but after you've treated your body as badly as I did for so long, you're bound to get inflammatory issues, hardcore. And I got them all.

Because of that, I can't eat those foods. And you know what? I would much prefer to not eat those foods because even if I wasn't allergic, they just mess with my mental health. The sugar come-downs, for example. Nobody's body can really process gluten, as much as everybody loves it, and I bet you that at least 98 per cent of people after they smash a burger say, 'Oh, I'm so full' or 'I'm so tired'. It's the gluten.

Most doctors would say to you, 'Cut that out.' And many, many naturopaths say that to you too. And if you can eat those things, good on you. I just can't.

So while I don't remember being overly scrutinised for gaining weight, I remember beating myself up mentally for it. And it's only now that I realise how different I looked, how completely different my face was, because I was so swollen from those things I shouldn't eat.

My eyes had shrunk. My mouth was different. It's just amazing what food can do to your body and mind. People hinted that I had had work done on my face because they were comparing how I looked then to how I look now. And I would say, 'Okay, well, there I was smashing gluten when I was a coeliac and I was drinking white wine, which makes you very bloated and swollen. I was extremely unhappy and I was just all-around swole and not in a good muscly way.' It wasn't 'having work done'. Don't get me wrong, I love a bit of cheeky Botox and filler, but not enough to completely alter my face. I just lost all that gluten weight and all that unhealthy swelling went away. I still have a little bit to go.

I'm not aiming at my previous weight, but that's mainly because I'm not interested in being 48 kilos. Even if I was 60 kilos I'd love it if it was muscle and from working hard. And I do get to treat myself with the things that I can eat. So I don't ever want to be too skinny again, or gain weight that's unhealthy, because when I'm at a healthy, happy weight, I feel good in my mind, body and spirit.

And on another note: I do know that women cop so much flack for gaining weight and I just don't know why it is anybody else's business. What you weigh is your business.

If you're unhappy and you're not eating right and you don't want to be the way you are, then that's something you can work on and I respect and appreciate that 100 per cent. And if you're having struggles with it, that's also understandable. We are so lucky to have access to all these beautiful foods.

It can be tough, but don't lose weight for anybody else. You do it for yourself. You do it for your mind and your body and your spirit. Don't let anyone bully you into thinking you should be a certain way because, especially in the industry I'm in, I feel like you can get subtle hints.

So don't let people do that to you. You be at the weight where you are healthy and comfortable, and what you weigh is nobody else's damn business. If they don't like it, they shouldn't look, darling. They just should not look.

CHAPTER 19

Endometriosis

I have mentioned before that I suffer from endometriosis. I was diagnosed with this a couple of years ago and because of it I had to go on the pill. I was always very anti-pill because I just didn't believe in any kind of medicine affecting my hormones and menstrual cycle. But because of the amount of pain I was in, and because I started to get adult acne again, my doctor highly recommended that I went on a very low dose of the pill, which I have done. It has helped with my skin and it has also helped with how severe my pain is.

But, again, I'm not a doctor so if you do have endometriosis and want to find out more information about this, make sure you contact your local GP. I can also highly recommend seeing a fabulous naturopath who focuses on endometriosis because there are plenty of them out there.

When I finish my next little work adventure, I will be seeing my naturopath about all things hormone related and getting off the pill. But before I start this next chapter of my life, there's no way I'd be messing with my hormones – because I could turn into a crazy person leading up to my period.

I would always suffer with terrible, terrible PMS, severe cramping, bloating like a little baby whale, acne, cravings out of this world, swollen sore breasts like you wouldn't believe. So I just thought, *There's gotta be a reason behind this.* The pain was unbearable.

I went to my doctor and she sent me to all the appropriate places to go and get checked up. I had an ultrasound and they couldn't find it, but the doctor said that didn't mean I didn't have endometriosis. So I still had to have the keyhole surgery and that was next level.

I legitimately have a phobia of belly buttons. My dad has this phobia too. It even has a name: omphalophobia.

Part of the keyhole surgery is that they enter through the belly button, which really freaked me out. The thought of the surgeon having to go right through my belly button ... I'm freakin' just writing that. Anyway, it meant that I had to completely prepare myself mentally for the procedure. I still went ahead with it, though, and they did end up finding a bit of endometriosis in there.

When you're diagnosed with endometriosis, this means that you need to have a very big change of life, otherwise it can grow back. (And most of the time it does. So I will probably need another check in a few years' time.)

So it's all about healthy lifestyle. There's an endometriosis diet that you can follow. A big, big no-no is drinking bulk alcohol, which I'm still learning to cut down on as I do like to have a drink while celebrating.

Mainly it's diet, though. Managing diet helps to keep the condition under control. You can find out about all the diets online or there's an endometriosis group on Facebook that you can join, which helps a lot with getting information if you're not aware of what's out there. Because, really, there's not a whole bunch of awareness.

It is getting better because so many women are diagnosed with endometriosis now, and it's so important to look after yourself, especially if you want to have children. So make sure you do speak to a professional. And don't feel ashamed if you have it. There's plenty of us out there and just join the groups, have a chat. Educate yourself – get amongst Google, get amongst the books, get a naturopath and read, read, read, read.

Get plenty of sleep, plenty of water, plenty of herbs, and reach out and chat to other people who have it – and always, always make sure you're listening to your body. If something doesn't sit right, then it generally isn't right. Your body is the best health and lie detector, so you use it. That's what it's there for.

CHAPTER 20

Meet the Real You

If you want to know the best way to get back to your true self, I highly recommend you go and live out in a jungle. I mean, if you can't do that it's totally fair enough. Not all of us are offered the opportunity to live in an African jungle for five weeks – as I was during *I'm a Celeb* – and be frightened out of our goddamn minds on the regular. But even if you can't do that, I highly recommend you take yourself out of society, somewhere else, for quite a solid amount of time.

There's something incredible about that feeling of going back to basics, where all you have is the clothes on your back, the fire to keep you warm, the food you are given and told when you can eat it, and the conversations you have in that environment.

You have nothing else; you're all equals in that situation. When you are stripped of all your vices and all your little bits and pieces that you feel define you, you really get to find out your truest self.

Believe it or not but your truest self isn't your fancy-ass car, or how big your fake boobs are, or how many followers you have on Instagram.

Your true self is how you connect with others in situations that you are not familiar with. How you handle being who you really would be if you didn't have all these things to distract you or to cover yourself or to hide behind.

So if you can't get to Africa, maybe just go outback in Australia. Just live off rice and beans. Go with a group of people so you can have some pure conversations about real stuff. Even if they're just shitty conversations they're still real because you're in the moment and the moment is all you got. You're not getting distracted by the latest iPhone or your friends and their dramas. You're just connecting with what's going on in the moment.

Go somewhere where you can find out who you really are again, because it is truly the best feeling in the entire world.

If I hadn't had that experience recently, I would never have been able to do the amount of things that have been thrown at me over the past few months. Before that I didn't know who the real Angie was anymore, but I do now, and I don't need to hide behind my vices all the time or distract myself with stuff that I used to distract myself with, like my phone or booze.

It's so nice to find your soul again. Our soul just gets hidden with whatever we can find to distract ourselves from getting to know our truest self. So get out there!

•

One thing that makes me really sad is the thought and the feeling of knowing that certain relationships and situations will never be the same again. You will never get to experience that exact moment ever again. I know it is a part of living and it's such a totally first-world problem, and I really do love change and love throwing myself into the most insane situations (clearly) because I do run off quite strong adrenaline.

If you felt the way I felt on the regular, I am more than sure you would probably ask yourself, 'How does this gal function?' But I do and I have managed to do it for twenty-nine years.

I just really get sad over the thought of not having relationships with people I used to have relationships with, and that I will never get that time back, and I just hope that I really didn't take that time I had with those people, or when I was in a particular environment that I loved, for granted.

Life just goes by so quick and we take so much stuff so seriously when really we should just be loving every single moment that we have because we are never going to get that time back.

That time you were sitting at your recently passed grandmother's house just having a cup of tea and feeling all the love – that's such a magic moment. Or that boyfriend you were with and you don't talk to him anymore but you just had the most beautiful time with him – that's not going to come back either.

Sometimes I think, *God, I love how time goes on and things change and evolve because that's life* – but I do wish good, solid relationships and friendships could last forever.

I had such a beautiful boyfriend when I was younger; he just taught me so much. But I think I wanted to be him more than be *with* him though. I loved him, but I wasn't in love. I wish we could have ended that relationship but kept our friendship and that he would share his life with me and I would share my life with him. But I guess that's not the way we work as humans sometimes.

For those of you who have stayed friends with every person you have dated or connected with in your time, kudos – I envy you. I have tried to rebuild friendships with ex-partners or old friends that I have drifted from, but then sometimes you just have to think everything happens for a reason and obviously those people aren't supposed to be in your life anymore or maybe just not at this time.

You shouldn't be sad that they are no longer there; instead be happy that you even got to have those times together. All good things come to an end.

It is so important for us humans to realise we can't get attached to moments, good or bad, because nothing lasts forever. That feeling of pure, pure bliss does not last forever; that feeling of utter sadness doesn't last forever either.

I have been down, down, deeper than down in the dumps and I would think to myself, *Holy shit balls, I am never going to be Angie again.* When you have that moment – or moments, if you are unlucky enough – where you feel you have lost your mind because you are just so incredibly depressed and anxious, you really learn not to take your normal self for granted. By normal self I mean, just to wake up and be grateful that you are feeling you and that you are no longer suffering. We sometimes take a healthy functioning mind for granted.

It's kind of like when you get a cold and you think, *I am never going to treat this temple of mine badly ever again* – but you will. Again and again. I sometimes still do take myself for granted and push the boundaries, but then I bring myself back to what is good and pure, and think how lucky I am to feel balanced. How lucky I am to be running off a bit of my average Angie anxiety but not be in that deep, deep depression where I can't eat or sleep and question everything I am doing.

I guess my point is that nothing lasts forever and even though it hurts at times, we can also be thankful that those breathtakingly awful moments won't last forever either. Enjoy it all, because eventually it all comes to an end. I don't want to say this to sound morbid, but it is true.

The one thing I know is that we all get out of here eventually. So don't mourn those bad situations either and think what a waste of a tank of gas dating old mate was, because I am sure he taught you something or you then met someone else really swell out of it, or you got to go on that sensational holiday to Malaysia (I may or may not be referring to personal experiences). Nothing like a good ol' trip down memory lane. Everything is an experience and a chance to grow.

You know what I reckon? I reckon we should all stop holding grudges. I believe that shit can cause cancer. When you hold on to something for too long and don't express yourself and feel it out, that right there is what causes all types of illnesses. It causes stuff inside of you to grow because you aren't allowing yourself to LET. IT. GO.

Everyone is just doin' what they can from his or her level of consciousness, so how about we stop holding on to grudges about those things we can't change.

We can't change how anybody reacts to someone else; all we can do is focus on how we handle situations. How we handle a negative situation says a lot about us and our character.

So just don't hold on to shit. Seriously, let it go. Stay in the moment and just hope for the best and hope that one day those people will find a higher level of consciousness too. We can't all vibe on the same frequency. If we were all the same, it would be mighty boring. So just do you, boo. Just do you.

CHAPTER 21

Pat on the Back

There have been plenty of times in my life where I have not given myself the pat on the back that I truly deserved. I bet most of you can relate to this.

Instead of patting myself on the back I would think, *Okay, what's next? What else can I do? Give me something next level to achieve!*

Sometimes I feel it is important to create a list of our achievements and be proud of what we have done to date.

For example, I always said I wanted to leave the Sunshine Coast and study drama, film and television. I graduated from high school and got a bloody good grade after being told that it would be almost impossible to move up from the average grade expected of me. But I improved my marks because I worked my butt off.

I am not one of those naturally smart people. I have to try very hard to get where I want to go or achieve the best result. I envy those naturally smart people or those people who are good at pretty much everything they do. Damn them and their good genes!

I didn't get the grade my best friend did and I would often compare myself to her when I should have focused on the fact my grade improved and given myself a massive pat on the back.

Again, at university I didn't pass with distinctions – but I passed every subject and got my Bachelor of Creative Industries Interdisciplinary. Pat on the back.

I had the ugliest little blue Holden Barina going around. Sometimes I was embarrassed to turn up to the fancy houses of the nannying jobs I had in Brisbane. But you know what? I worked my butt off to save my pennies to get that little piece of shit so, again, pat on the back for me.

I also worked my butt off at university to get high enough grades to be able to study over in California at San Jose State University, and I learnt more in that one semester abroad than I did in my entire degree back home in Australia. Not to mention I had the best time ever making friends across the globe.

Another recommendation high on my list is that if you can, most definitely study abroad. It was truly one of the best life experiences I have ever had. The different culture, learning in a country where film/TV is their jam, the characters you meet, the travel you get to do … and my god, the frat parties – YAS!

I worked hard in my studies to reach the level needed to be even accepted to study abroad and then I worked every day I wasn't at uni as a nanny or childcare worker to save up my spending and travel money. But I was very lucky that my family acknowledged my hard work and set me a goal: if I got the grades and saved up the amount of money I needed then my dad would cover the cost of study/on campus living – winning!

I could sit here for days and ramble on about all my achievements, big or small, but I don't want to look like I'm a raving, self-absorbed asshole. The point of this is to be proud of all your achievements. If you have put in the hard yards, the hours, the effort and dedicated your precious time to something and achieved it, good on you. Remember to give yourself a pat on the back.

Relish the moment after you reached your goal. Don't say, 'Okay, well, I nailed that so what is next?' I know I have done that too many times because I am such a pusher. I always wanted more for myself because maybe I didn't feel like what I was doing was enough, and that's, well, just a little bit sad. We aren't what we do or what we have.

With saying that, though, it doesn't mean we can't be proud of what we do and what we have – just don't let it define you or consume you.

Be proud of all you do, big or small. Keep kicking them goals.

CHAPTER 22

Living Abroad

I have been blessed enough to live in two different countries already. As I mentioned earlier, I studied and lived in San Jose, California, when I was nineteen, and completed a semester of my degree there. Best time of my life. Highly recommend it. Pop him on your list.

Then there was London. Beautiful, busy, charming yet soul-sucking London.

I have had some of my best times in London and some of my worst. I don't think it was London's fault. Other than the fact it is expensive as all hell to live the high life. I did choose two of the most expensive cities in the world to set up shop in for just under two years.

I think my idea of living between London and Sydney was my fault. I mean, who do I think I am? The freakin' Queen? I didn't even have enough money to support myself in Sydney let alone to and from Sydney and London.

Bless me and my need to push myself to the limit and the lengths I will go to find happiness! You've got to give me credit for that: I am relentless. I would probably do it all over again, to be honest. Just with an endless sum of money from somewhere unknown to me.

London is the bee's knees, London is the cat's pyjamas. Especially when your best friend in the world lives there. I could do a whole chapter on Sarah (my best friend) but I don't know if that would be weird or not. Sarah can just feature throughout this chapter.

Sarah is my best friend and soul sister. To give you a wee background story on her so she isn't this random name I throw out from time to time: we met when we were thirteen when she moved from the Philippines to the Sunshine Coast. I mean, come on! How magic is that! Out of all the places in the world, her dad sent her and her two sisters and mum right to my stomping ground?! Ahhh, thank you, universe.

Sarah is my family. Her sisters are my family. Her mum and dad are my second mum and dad. I love them. Sarah and I moved to Brisbane together and studied there; we went to San Jose together to study; and then she moved to London and I moved to Sydney. To say I was devastated is an understatement – BUT wait, it gets better. Sarah spent a year in London when we first graduated from university and realised that London was a bitch of a place to live with no money, so she moved to Sydney! Ahhh, the world made sense yet again.

We had what I believe to be three to four magical years together in Sydney and then, nup, London wins again. Sarah has been there ever since and worked her little butt off and now she lives the dream. That's me gal right there.

Okay, back to what I was originally talking about – and that was not Sarah, but I am a sicko and needed to sneak her and her magical soul in here one way or another.

Living in London was tough and glorious. I think I have 'lived' there maybe four times, if my memory serves me right. I would crash wherever Sarah was, for months on end. But the last time I did London I was an au pair and I lived like a big gal with the family I worked for.

I was a nanny for two babies under two. Don't do it. Don't get me wrong, beautiful family and amazing life experience – but two under two? Hot diggity damn, what was I thinking? Two under two is like having little stray kittens on speed. You just love them but also want to lock yourself in a room and rock backwards and forwards in the foetal position. Or maybe that was just me and the state I was in at the time. That sweet, sweet run-off-her-feet, feeling-like-she-is-about-to-have-a-breakdown state.

This state is almost second nature to me, isn't it? By the end of this book y'all will think that's just me, a bloody mad woman.

Now I think of it, I am still living ludicrously. Oh well, what are you going to do, hey? Ya live and ya learn. In my case I mainly just live.

Kidding! I have learnt A LOT. It's all about practice, my babies. I'll get there.

Anyway, back to London. The beauty of living in London is that you can travel to pretty much any nearby country on your weekends off. I mean, that just makes everything better, right? I have travelled through so much of Europe and have met some of the best people in my life. All that saving and struggle is well worth it.

If I could offer any advice, though, it would be to maybe not live between two of the most expensive cities at the same time. Unless you're the spawn of Beyoncé or a Kardashian child or you have some kind of money tree – in which case, by all means get amongst it. But if you are a basic bitch like me and have to work ya butt off to make a living, then maybe just give yourself a little time. Move back to the family home, if that is an option, and save some money.

Or when you get to London just stay there and do not come home every three months to film a television show. Not ideal for the ol' bod. That flight from Australia to England is a bitch once in a blue moon, and I was doing it on the regular.

I believe living in another country does come with its challenges that you may not experience just sitting at home and plodding along. There are struggles with that, though, too, aren't there? Wherever you go there will be challenges and hurdles, but I believe that nothing worth it comes easy. I would actually rather live between two of the most expensive cities in the world rocking shingles just before a 32-hour flight than to have stayed put and lived life plodding along. But hey, that's just not my character. I think each to their own.

My friends hate it but that is one of my favourite sayings of all time: each to their damn own. If you like the simple life then keep doing you. I almost envy people who can be content with living in the same place their whole life and working the same nine-to-five forever, but that is just not me. I am a wild, crazy life-wishing gypsy.

One day that may calm down, but for now the universe seems to keep firing these absolute cannonballs at me and I just keep jumping right on them like some kind of joy-ride sicko.

CHAPTER 23

South Africa and SEED

One of my greatest achievements came in early 2018, when I was asked to travel to South Africa to be a part of SEED.

SEED is a multi-faceted educational program dedicated to bringing social awareness, self-empowerment and life skills to high-risk teenage girls in South Africa.

I know, right? Say no more! But I will anyway.

This was next-level dream-come-true status. I had just got back to Sydney after being in Queensland for the Christmas period, filming had started for *Gogglebox* and I had no money (again) – but guess what ... You probably guessed it: home girl made it work just like she always does, with only a few mental breakdowns along the way. Wooooo! Go get it, girl.

See, I can look back now and laugh at the moments I felt like were some of my worst, when really they are just pretty little tales to tell my new friends (you readers) and to acknowledge how far I have come and the absolute experiences I got to have along the way. Magic moment!

Because filming for *Gogglebox* had started, the trip was going to be tricky. We filmed every week, twice a week, for eight to nine weeks, and the SEED camp landed towards the end of filming. Scheduling was always a nightmare because the production company had to consider all the other Sydney families on the show, and most schedules had been approved at the beginning of filming.

(If I could do a chapter about scheduling and how that screwed up most of my life last year I totally would, but I also don't want to look like a resentful cow. I will just put that on my 'things I need to let go of' list.)

Anyway, this time round the scheduling gods were on my side. At least the universe did have my back! Once again!

I managed to sneak in a quick trip to Gauteng, which is a northern province of South Africa. The name means 'place of gold' and gold is exactly what I found during my seven-day trip.

The flight was eighteen-plus hours. I had one day in Johannesburg to get over the hectic jet lag and then the next day we headed off to Orange Farm in Gauteng. Orange Farm is a township located approximately 45 kilometres from Johannesburg.

It was nothing like I have ever seen before. Orange Farm is undeveloped and the challenges that are faced by the community are caused by ridiculously high levels of poverty. I don't like to talk too much about a place I only shared less than a week with, but the state of it broke my heart. The people are so magical and deserve so much more than how they are living.

During my time at the second SEED camp at the Zonkizizwe elementary school in Orange Farm, I got to know around eighteen young ladies from the ages of ten to eighteen. Their smiles warmed my heart and their hearts were as big as the universe.

The five-day program incorporated wellness, self-empowerment and entrepreneurship. I was there to teach storytelling through performance or any creative outlet they saw fit.

When I wasn't teaching my class, I was involved in all the other workshops and got to listen to the entrepreneur guests who came and taught the girls about work ethic and their experiences creating their own businesses and breaking the strong and traditional gender ideologies.

Being a woman in Orange Farm is more than hard: most women end up pregnant at a very young age and don't have any of the opportunities we do here in Australia.

The girls worked their little butts off during camp. For the majority of them, this was their first experience outside of school or home and a look into the business world. The girls also got to explore the benefits of yoga and meditation.

We gave them the space to feel safe and to dream. To share their experiences and know that they are strong, independent women who can overcome all these obstacles if they work together.

By the end of the week the girls had created their very own products including natural skincare, recycled fashion and beaded jewellery.

The final day of the camp – which I had to miss due to filming – was a pop-up market that they put on for their local community. It was the chance to show off their products and make some cash.

In my class we made up a performance that the girls would do at the beginning of the market. I wasn't there but I heard it was solid gold.

My final day with the girls was devastating. They sang me a thousand songs, they danced, they gave me notes telling me how they would never forget me and wished I would come back soon. I cried, they cried. We all cried.

That week was short but it was more than sweet. I left feeling every single goosebump on my body and with a full heart.

Mumma Africa is indescribable. As soon as you land there, you feel as though you are back in the motherland.

The people, the food, the culture – just pure bliss. One day, after the madness of this year, I will be back with my little South African princesses. Some of us still keep in touch via Facebook. Others, I will just have to wait until we cross paths again and I can give them a big heart-to-heart cuddle.

Be blessed for the opportunities we have here in Australia as young women. I know we are not 100 per cent there yet, but we have so much more support and safety then these girls from Orange Farm do. Let's take the time to be grateful for what we do have and then hope with that gratitude more opportunity and love for all women and men across the world will grow. I think the simple way to put it is: EQUALITY FOR ALL!

CHAPTER 24

In the Flow

A state of mind I have recently adopted is to be able to go with the flow.

Since last year to this year, life has changed so much I sometimes have to pinch myself. 2018 was one of my lowest points, hands down. I could hardly afford a ticket home to visit my sick Nanny let alone afford health appointments and gym memberships to keep myself feeling and looking great.

(I also believe that when you look great, you feel great. When you feel great within, you also look great. They go hand in hand, really.)

This year I have experienced things I actually laugh about. Never in a million years would I have dreamed up what I have had presented to me. Cars come to pick me up from and drop me off to beautiful hotels in Sydney and Melbourne. I have had business-class trips to South Africa. I have stylists and make-up artists and dresses being designed specifically for me.

For me? This little lass who was born in Nambour Hospital in 1990 with a head the shape of a cone. *ME?*

Sometimes I get so frightened of this drastic change. I think, *When will it come crumbling down?* Surely it has to, as it is too good to be true.

Maybe I need to change that mind frame, though, and think, *Hey, maybe I deserve this right now in my life. This is what the universe wants for me.* Appreciate and accept and be grateful.

I have worked hard since I was legally allowed to. I have always put my family first and have helped everyone I love when in need. I have literally slept in my own car when I didn't have a home and sometimes I could not even afford to go to the doctor.

Don't get me wrong, I don't think I'm fancy as all f*ck now that I occasionally get free shit and stay in nice places. I'm certainly not going to get used to this lush life because the lushness is not me.

These things do not define me as a person. Nor will I ever *expect* that I deserve this. I haven't changed at all.

I still rock around in my brother's old sweaters and buy cheap shoes and hang out with my same friends. I spend most of my free time hanging with my family and visiting my Nan. There isn't anything boujee about this gal.

I also realise this could all end as quickly as it began. This is part of the flow. Life can be so low and then have these complete highs and people tend to get carried away with the highs and forget to stay grounded and humble. When the lows hit, they think, *This is it, this must be what life is.*

Nothing stays the same. Good or bad. It helps to be mindful and to go with the flow. Sounds so clichéd and lame, doesn't it?

Imagine, though, accepting what is happening right now and not trying to manipulate it or change it. Not always needing the answers. Just simply go with the flow and trust that this is where you need to be in this very moment.

Give it a red-hot go. Really, when you truly think about it, what is there to lose? All we got is time. So try going with the flow.

CHAPTER 25

Gogglebox

When Yvie and I were first asked to do *Gogglebox*, we said, 'Oh my god, that sounds like the biggest joke.' Watching people watch television for a living – who even thought of that, number one, and number two, who would actually say *yes* to audition for that? But we did.

How it all started was that one of Yvie's best friends was the post-producer for Blake Garvey's season of *The Bachelor*. He got an internal email from Shine Endemol, the production company that makes *Gogglebox*, because at the time Shine were producing the *Bachelor* franchise.

The email said, 'Do you know anybody who loves to watch television and who has an opinion?' And he was, like, 'Do I ever!'

Without even asking us first, he sent off a video of Yvie, Tom and me just doing our usual crazy thangs, carrying on like two-bob watches, probably singing some kind of song and being super inappropriate.

A week later we got a call from the *Gogglebox* casting director saying, 'Do you want to audition for this show?' And we were like, 'This is absolutely ludicrous. Probably not.'

But ... Yvie and I are also massive believers that if things pop up, it's a sign from the universe. So just give it a try and go from there.

So we decided to do the audition. It was via Skype and the person auditioning us showed us a picture of Barack Obama, who was then president of the United States, and showed us a picture of Tony Abbott because he was the current prime minister, and a picture of a reality star who was popular at that time, and we would just have to talk to each other and say what we thought and felt about that person.

That was the audition. Wait – there were actually a couple of those.

I was booked to go travelling in the Philippines for three months with my best friend, Sarah. I was so excited to be going there, because it already felt like my second home after growing up with Sarah and hearing all about the place, and knowing her best friends, I was so excited to finally meet her Filipino family.

Then Yvie and I got a call really close to when I was about to leave, saying, 'You two are the first to be cast in the show and we've kind of cast it around you. You're such strong characters for the show and we would love to have you be a part of it.'

And we said, 'Okay, well, that's our sign – we'll give it a go.'

We watched the UK season of *Gogglebox* and then we heard it had won BAFTA awards and so many other awards, and that it was one of the highest-rating shows in the UK.

So we thought, *You never know: Australia, even though it has massive tall poppy syndrome and usually shit-cans every new television show that comes on, may like this one. Let's just do it. Seems like it's done well in the UK.*

Let's hope for the best and expect the worst – that was our motto.

Then the first episode aired and people just loved it. It picked up an audience so quickly.

We originally did it because we'd just started rescuing and fostering dogs, and we loved Paws and Recover. So we figured that we could just talk about rescue dogs for the reality part of the show when we weren't watching TV. Because they often showed a lot of reality.

So we would involve the dogs all the time. We always had a different dog on the couch and the audience went absolutely mad for it. They adored it. They loved that we were two single girls with a seventeen-year age gap living together in the inner west of Sydney, rescuing all these dogs, always having a different dog on the couch. And we lived with a man with Down syndrome.

We were the ultimate modern family. That's what we called ourselves when we were down at the park. When it was me, Yvie, Tom and a pack of rescue dogs, we'd say, 'Are we not the ultimate modern family? Look at us go!'

We figured that if one episode could make one person rescue a dog, then we'd done our job – but then it just went up and beyond our wildest dreams.

Yvie and I stayed on *Gogglebox* for eight seasons – four years. I had my twenty-fourth birthday on there and I left just before my twenty-ninth birthday. We won three Logies, and we were up for other awards as well. And without *Gogglebox* I never would be doing what I'm doing right now. I probably wouldn't be writing a book that people actually want to read. (Although I would still be writing anyway because I do love it.) I wouldn't have been on *I'm a Celebrity ... Get Me Out of Here!* I wouldn't have met half of the amazing people I've met.

I'm so grateful for *Gogglebox* and everything that the show has done for me, but it comes to a stage in anyone's life, in any job, where you think, *I've learnt all I can learn about myself and this job; there's really nothing more I can gain from this experience.*

We helped rehome and rescue that many dogs. We promoted #adoptdontshop. We got to be two women in Australia with such solid opinions speaking out to other women who probably thought, *You never see women allowed to carry on like that on television and get away with it.* But we did for four years, twice a year for ten weeks in a row. That was just something so magical for me, knowing that I was a woman and I could say my opinions and people actually tuned in to watch me talk about something. It could be a renovation show or a reality show, but we would speak about really serious issues too and we'd watch documentaries that really touched our hearts, and we cried and we were vulnerable.

We allowed the Australian public into our home. Not physically but metaphorically and emotionally. They got to grow with us over those four years, and we experienced a lot of loss over those four years. Yvie lost her mum. I lost my Poppy and my Nanny all while I was on that show. We lost a lot of rescue dogs. And because it's such a family show, people get really attached to you and they go through that process with you.

They knew when we were sick because we couldn't film. And we had so many people wishing us to get better. It was like a real little community.

So leaving *Gogglebox* was not an easy decision, but when all signs are pointing to getting the hell out of Sydney and to being with your family, you've got to listen and you've got to trust your gut. Bad things kept happening because I kept ignoring my gut.

But I'm very, very grateful for *Gogglebox* and everything that I experienced with it throughout the four years, and everything that's come after it, and it has just been absolutely mind blowing.

We originally thought the show was a bit of a laugh, but we wanted to give it a red-hot go. And it was never hard to come up with things to say because Yvie and I bounced off each other so swimmingly at the beginning. By the end I think we might have acted a little bit, but it was still us. We were forcing ourselves to be the same people over the last four years but really we had loved, lost, grown and felt we needed a change.

It could feel invasive, too, because the cameras and the audience were in our house. We had that many dogs. We lived with Tom. We were constantly stopping to check Tom's blood levels with him being a diabetic or to clean up one of the dog's spews. So it did get quite overwhelming in the sense that it wasn't a normal house. It was a full-on hectic lifestyle home where we were caring for many things and people other than ourselves.

By the end I think we lost our spark a little bit. We became a little bit too comfortable – and what more can you really say after four years of watching similar shows over and over? I think we had given it our all and we'd run out of our tank of gas and it was time for them to bring new people in.

Change is good. You don't want to watch the same people watching TV forever if they aren't fully invested anymore. It's nice to spice things up; keep the old faithfuls in because everybody loves them and can relate to them, and then bring in some new spice. What's more exciting than spice in your life?

I know we definitely changed from the first episode of season one to the last of season eight. At the beginning it was probably a creative exercise because Yvie and I are creative people, but over the years it became almost like breathing. It was just so familiar to us. I think we got lazier and we just got more comfortable, so we probably got more inappropriate as time went on.

At the start I was probably a little bit more polite and trying not to offend anyone. And by the end I'm pretty sure I said I wanted to sleep with the prime minister of Australia at the time! Which is pretty hardcore and not something you really want your friends and family to hear you say. But I said it and they showed it. So what are you going to do? Verbal diarrhoea is something I suffer from.

We loved the way people responded to the show – everybody felt like they were our friends. But it did become more like a job. We'd lost the zest and passion for it, and that show deserves to have people with zest and passion because it's such an amazing show.

When we started realising that we saw it as more of a chore because things had started to change in our personal lives – we were a little bit more out of control – we didn't want to become a burden, so it was a good time for us to leave.

There were some days when we would watch shows and I would actually not say anything. I would sit down on the couch and think, *I'm not putting on a show today. I'm not in a good mood and I don't care for this television program at all. And Angie watching television would never watch this program.* So, really, if I'd said anything it would just be me being fake. And I'm very adamant about staying true to myself and being real. But that meant sometimes I would just sit there and be a massive baby and not say anything at all.

We could usually rely on the dogs for a bit of drama, though. I don't think any of them misbehaved badly, although Leo could be tricky. He was Yvie's pride and joy who passed away a couple of years ago. I dreaded that day coming and then it happened and it was just absolutely heartbreaking. I remember I was at my

Nanny Fae's house when Yvie called and told me she had to put Leo down and I was hysterical. Nanny sent Yvie a beautiful letter saying he's in a better place and he's up there with the other dogs and all. I was just so sad because I knew how much Yvie's heart was breaking and I always feel her feels so heavily.

But Leo, he used to attack me on the couch. I'd be sitting there watching TV and Yvie would get up to get us a drink or something to eat and I'd move Leo over and he'd turn around and try to attack me. I would scream bloody murder. My naughty soul brother.

A lot of the time the dogs would just drop their guts while we were filming and it would stink so bad and that reality would be in the show, which was so great because you got to see a couple of nutcases with all their wild hounds that they just loved so much and who loved us as well.

I'm pretty sure one of the dogs threw up on us while we were filming, or I sat in the remnants of some dog poo because the dog did a poo outside and it was still hanging from their bum.

We often sang songs about the dogs which would also make it to air. Once Leo was humping a pillow and Yvie and I made up a song about it – we were rapping, actually – and that made it to air. And it was just fabulous. This little feral Pomeranian humping the absolute hell out of a pillow and two girls rapping to the dog humping.

We had so many good times on that couch. So many good times with our dogs, being able to be ourselves, talking about the big issues of the world and talking absolute dross. What better job to have, really, with your best mate.

I'm very blessed for my time on *Gogglebox*. I wouldn't change a thing.

CHAPTER 26

I'm a Celeb

I have to admit that going into the jungle for *I'm a Celebrity ... Get Me Out of Here!* was one of the best things to have happened to me after the year that was 2018. That experience was heaven sent.

I got to be stripped of my vices and completely and utterly vulnerable amongst people who are known as 'somebodies' in the outside world – but in the jungle we were all equals. There was no hierarchy at all.

Don't get me wrong, it was incredibly hard to wake up around twelve or so other people who I would generally not dream of letting see me with no make-up and be as dirty and grubby as I was. Not to mention the hundreds of cameras that are on you 24/7. That was so overwhelming for me.

The thought of sleeping next to a bunch of strangers was enough to set off my anxiety. I went in as a bag of nerves. And I left feeling the best I have felt probably in my entire life. Big call, right, but I reckon it's right up there as one of the best feelings of my life.

I had to leap right in; there was no real preparation for a show like that. You could watch old seasons and just shit yourself with nerves thinking, *How would I be with snakes? Or eating that? Or dealing with that person?* The fear of the unknown was absolutely next level.

I had one severe panic attack the night that my minder took my phone off me. Not because I couldn't check my socials but because I was generally in control of that. Having a phone is such a creature comfort. The thought that I no longer had the choice to pick up the phone and speak to my mum or listen to my favourite meditation apps sent me into a wild trip of pure anxiety all night long.

I remember I had to get up at 1.30 a.m. That was our wake-up call for the first episode shoot where Yvie and I had to somewhat '*Gogglebox*' the camp mates walking in for their first day.

I reckon I had an hour's sleep in between the manic anxiety sessions. I was exhausted. Then I had to perform for god knows how many hours that day.

I then managed to have another little panic attack right before we got our blindfolds taken off and were released into a camp in the African jungle that we had never seen before. Except, of course, on our TV screens, when Yvie and I were in shock about what these celebrities had to go through on this very show we had now signed up for. Madness. From couch potatoes in our comfort zones to absolute fresh jungle babies completely out of their comfort zones. So very far away from home and all our good things in life.

The first day of being in the camp was a blur. It is safe to say I was a BON (that's 'bag of nerves'). But surprisingly no one had any idea at all that I was shitting bricks left right and centre. I am quite good at hiding the utter fear that consumes my entire body. Practice makes perfect, I guess. 'Fake it till you make it' is another one of my faves.

But I highly recommend leaping into the void! I had no preparation for this show. I could not think about it because it would freak me out too much or send my mind wild. Thinking of not being able to talk to my nearest and dearest for five weeks and have all my control taken off me was super scary. And I absolutely loved it.

It took me a wee while but once I was settled I was in my absolute element. I was officially a little grubby jungle baby who now totally dug the simple things in life. I worked out quickly that I really am quite the simpleton.

I had this new-found appreciation for food and knowing what the time was and being able to do whatever I wanted in the real world. We really take those types of things for granted. Trust me. When they are taken from you, you truly do miss them so much and promise yourself you will never take them for granted again. But you do. As humans we forget very easily, which is a bit of a bummer.

Being so raw and vulnerable opens you up to way more criticism too. But I enjoyed myself so much in the jungle and found the real Angie again, so I really didn't give a diggity damn what those keyboard warriors out there had to say.

I knew who I was again and what I had been through and I never broke. I have had some hectic *breakdowns* (never in the jungle, surprisingly – the only tears I shed in there were pure tears of joy and happiness) but even during the heaviest and most vulnerable periods of my life they have never broken me. For that I am very proud of myself.

Opinions are like assholes: everybody has got one, and that is never going to change. So now I just do me knowing that I have a heart of gold and a mind that is always eager to learn and change and dream. That is what the jungle was for me. All those feels.

I would do it again in a heartbeat.

CHAPTER 27

Looking for Love? How About Loving Yourself!

Love. The big four-letter word that looks and sounds so sweet and innocent but really scares the absolute crapola out of most of us. Can I get an amen?

I certainly know it has scared the life out of me for a long time. It still kind of does, to some degree.

It is safe to say that I have not looked for love in a long time. I have been single for eight years now, and this is by choice.

Of course, this has been hard at times. Sometimes I have felt so lonely and dated the wrong people to fill that void, and those wrong people have really taken advantage of my kindness. But I also understand that I am no walk in the park, either, when I am in a mood.

Plus, even though they took advantage of my kindness I also took advantage of them and really was only using them to fill that void – which isn't really nice, either, is it? Knowing they are not the one but still wanting them around.

I know my bad behaviour so well. Sometimes I don't know whether that is a good thing or a bad thing. Being so self-aware is great, but being self-aware and still doing what you shouldn't do … does that make me a genius or a monster? I will let you individually decide on that one. I guess that answer could be left in the eye of the beholder.

But, yes, being single for so long wasn't always sunshine and rainbows, especially when I lost my Nanny Fae last year. I saw a lot of my cousins with their partners and it made me think how nice it would have been for me to have had someone special to turn to.

It sometimes breaks my heart to think that I will never get to introduce my Nanny Fae to my soul mate. Although now I know that I will most certainly find one with her up there working her sweet angel magic.

The main reason behind me being single was that I had not loved myself in such a long time, and I am a massive believer in truly, madly, deeply loving yourself before you expect someone else to love you. We spend so much time looking for this ideal partner when we should be looking at *ourselves* to be that ideal partner.

Sounds so simple, doesn't it? Well, why the hell don't more of us do it, then? We also spend so much time with ourselves yet we have no real idea who we are – what on earth is that all about?!

People seem to spend more time ignoring the fact they really should love themselves first, really get to know themselves first, before expecting someone else to 'get them' and especially not to expect someone else to solve their problems and make their life better.

I have watched so many people go from partner to partner, and yet they are always unhappy and find a way to blame it on the person they are with. I'm like, 'Home girl (or boy), have ya checked in with yourself lately? Do you even know who YOU are?'

Filling a void with love, attention or affection – whatever it is we search for to get that feeling we all seem to crave from a significant other – isn't the answer, in my book. I say this because I have done it and it was awful. I have seen it and it is awful to witness.

Sometimes we need to stop putting so much pressure on looking for love in someone else or something else. We have SO much of that sweet, sweet love around us and inside of us at all times.

The love I have for my family, my friends and my dogs is so pure and real, along with that love I know I can have for myself, and now I know when the time is right, when the universe sees fit, I have all this love inside of me for a special someone!

It just took me time to feel again, and to really get to know myself and be more than okay with who I am. That I am deserving and ready for love.

I have had so many life experiences, ticked so many boxes on my list of what I wanted to do by myself before I shared my life with someone else.

I am so content with myself that I know I can happily be single. But for once, I don't want to be.

I don't need a partner – I want one.

I can't believe I am saying that out loud for the first time. What a nice realisation I have come to in my own time, never letting society get in my head.

Remember, though: you never *need* someone. You can want someone but once you get into that need mind frame, well, that is a different ball game. We're going to have to turn to Oprah for that one.

I am not qualified to be offering advice in the 'need department'. Just trust me when I say, you don't need anyone to make you happy. You've just got to really start looking within and loving number one!

CHAPTER 28

Dating Down

I have definitely dated some questionable gents in my time, but with saying that I don't look back and cringe and think, *Ewww, why did I date them?* (Okay, I do a little bit.)

Mainly I look back and think, well, if I didn't date that person, or hang out with that person, or be with that person in some way, then I wouldn't really know what I don't want in a partner.

Try to see silver linings after you date a numpty. Plus, I read somewhere that every single person who comes into your life is meant to come into your life for a reason – we learn something from that experience.

If you have dated a massive douchebag, then you know for your next partner that if you see the same or similar qualities, you're not going to stick around, because you have already dated one of those and know they are not for you.

That's what your younger years are for: to date different types of people and learn what you do like and what you don't like. You can then make a mental note that you really did like a particular quality in that person, but not how that person handles something else, etc., etc. So that the next time you hope the upcoming partner has all those good qualities you found in dating an array of people.

Another thing I thought about what happened to me last year was that I was dating this guy around the time that I felt like everything important in my life was leaving. A lot of things were coming to an end for me. It started off with losing my Poppy, then giving up my home in Sydney because I was trying so hard to be a normal house-renting human who stays put, losing my Nanny, leaving *Gogglebox*, leaving Sydney to move back home to Queensland – and then he and I stopped hanging out (we were never official due to me having serious commitment issues and still feeling I had more to achieve as a single soul searcher).

He then ended up with someone else literally a week later! What a kick in the dick that was!

Even though I didn't want to make things official, I didn't think that the time we spent with each other was so easy to get over that he could end up with another woman a week later.

My heart and mind were in a shambles. I thought to myself, firstly, why in the name of Beyoncé did he invest so much time into this relationship or whatever it was he had with me? Going on about how much he thought I was the one and how everything aligned so perfectly, and then a week later he was with an old love?

Why did I continue hanging out with this person when I knew he was not the one and it wasn't going to work out? He was ready and rearing to settle down and I wasn't. I still wanted to do my own thing.

I felt in my loins that something else or something more was coming. Lucky I trusted that feeling, because leaving Sydney was the best decision I had made in a long time.

I finally listened to the universe and let go of all the safety nets that I kept falling back into for many years because I was so frightened to see what else was out there.

Uncertainty stops us from doing so much in our lives when uncertainty is really the only thing we should be certain about. Just go with the flow of life. Let go of that control.

I often thought, *What if it isn't going to be anything like I thought it would be?* But letting go offered so much more than I ever thought it would.

After I let go of the fear of the unknown and left Sydney and said goodbye to a show which was my comfort zone for years, everything fell into place. Yvie,

Tom and I had an escape trip to Bali and within the first week of our trip we had a call from the producers of *I'm a Celebrity* asking us to be on the show ... TOGETHER! That show was hands down one of the best experiences of my life. I don't care what none of y'all think about that call – unless you have lived it, it's far too hard to explain. I know some people hated it, but not this gal.

That experience was exactly what I needed. I needed to be stripped of everything and to be completely out of my comfort zone, away from all my vices that I relied on to numb the pain, and to be away from all the pain that I had endured over the last six months, to know who I really was again.

With all of this being taken away and having nothing to hide behind, I got to know Angie and I really quite liked her. I'd missed her.

After the show, coming back to reality this year has been amazing with all the opportunities that have been presented to me.

Becoming the Bachelorette is going to be an experience where I get to find out more about myself and date and be really open to dating for the first time. That is so frightening to me but such a magic moment too.

To be vulnerable is a gift, not something to see as a weakness, and I am learning more about that with every experience that comes my way.

Let's back it up a little and go back to the dude I was talking about earlier. After it was over and he moved on so quickly, I thought, *What did I learn from this?* I was so hurt. I originally pushed him away but as soon as he found someone else I was, like, NO, this can't be another situation in my life that comes to an end.

Ah humans, always wanting what we can't have.

It was too late, because he had found someone who was just as keen to settle down as he was, and I look back now and I totally respect that. At the time I didn't because I was absolutely punched in the guts by rejection and was stuck in the whole 'why me' phase.

I am so grateful for that experience because it opened my heart up to knowing that I could actually be vulnerable with a man again, and that I could actually feel for someone. Even though he wasn't the right someone, I still had that feeling there that I had not felt in such a long time. Even though he didn't end up being the one, it was an experience to let me know that I am ready to open my heart to someone, I am ready to share my life with a fella and hopefully find my ... soul mate!

Yeah, I said it! I'm one of those people now and I am not even mad, I'm impressed.

On a side note, I do believe we have more than one soul mate out there. We have soul mates for different parts of our life. If I end up with one soul mate and it doesn't work out, I'm not going to be completely and utterly heartbroken because I now know that the relationship and the time we spend together is going to be another lesson in life that could potentially open up more doors to the next chapter – and so far these doors I have been opening since learning lessons have been some pretty sensational doors.

After experiencing so much loss last year, I have realised even more so how BIG my heart is and how much it can love, and the person who gets to share my heart with me is one lucky person. Because when I love, I love hard out! Just ask any of my friends, family members or rescue dogs. If them rescue dogs could talk, they would tell you a thing or two about this big heart of mine, and they would probably also tell you how freakin' annoying I am with all the baby talk and pashes to the face they get.

Hot damn, let's hope I don't do that to the person I end up with because I would be the biggest hypocrite in the world. I have only voiced my opinion on baby talk and public displays of affection in a negative way – I will not be surprised at how amazing it is that one can probably change very quickly when they find that special someone. So I should have really kept my big mouth shut. I will, however, be the first to eat my own words if I do turn out to be one of those baby-talkin' romancers I cursed at.

All those endings last year made for new beginnings. Which sounds super clichéd but it's so true. Once I accepted all the endings, my life started to fall into place.

I have not felt this good in so long. It is almost like I have gone back to being a child, when the fear of the unknown doesn't exist and people's opinions haven't affected me yet. Remember those days? Those days were bliss.

Even though I have no control over my life at the moment, I love it. I wake up and I do whatever I am told to do, which is a completely new experience for me. Whether that be by my manager, by my work or by the universe, I wake up and I say, 'Today I'm going to write', or 'Today I am going to work out', or 'Today I am flying to Sydney to film, tomorrow I am flying to Melbourne.' I don't wig out about it, either – I just think, *Yeah, okay, that's what I have to do, that's what the universe wants me to do right now.*

I am meeting some amazing people along the way, which is just great – to me that's what life is all about. I think making connections is why we are put on this planet. I'm not even talking about romantic connections, I'm talking all connections. That shit is what makes the world go round.

My connections come from the opportunities I get to be around people and make them laugh, to make them happy, offer them some Angie advice. Or for people to make me happy, laugh and offer me words of wisdom that I can take on board in this life of mine. I just love that.

That's my favourite thing in the world. Just going about life, having experiences and making connections.

So you keep dating those questionable dudes until you find the right one, and you keep hanging out with those questionable friends because, at the end of the day, it is all an experience. And you can look back and tell the grandkids, or ya little mates at the retirement village over happy hour, your tale about finding all these soul mates and the questionable experiences you have had.

You would assume that since I have been so anti-relationships and quite anti-men most of my adult life that I must have had a dreadful dating history with men. I must have had a relationship mess me up real good.

The truth is, I really have not. If anything, I have been absolutely spoilt for choice. I did peak early. My first boyfriend was a dreamboat who taught me so much. He took me on my first trip overseas, to Thailand. He waited two whole years to have sex with me because I did not want any sexy time while I was still at school. This was just something I had in my mind and once I have a belief I'm quite adamant about seeing it through. I didn't want to mix sex with study. If I wasn't mature enough to have a baby then I wasn't mature enough to be having sex.

I lost my virginity to him on my eighteenth-birthday trip to Thailand, on Valentine's Day. Disgustingly romantic or what?

My second boyfriend paid for my entire trip to Malaysia to go and meet his mum and dad in Kuala Lumpur. We travelled to islands around Malaysia and I was treated like a queen.

My third boyfriend paid for absolutely everything and bought me the most insane gifts without me ever hinting or asking. He was kind and adored me so much I felt it, and it was rather overwhelming.

I had a beautiful doctor come into my life and even before our first date he flew me business class to surprise-visit my mum for Mother's Day, because anyone who knows me knows how much my mum and I mean to one another. The doctor also came to Sydney for a weekend and treated me to trips to the zoo, concerts and the best hotel in Sydney, and constantly bent over backwards to make me laugh.

I had a passionate Greek man offer to start selling drugs in Mykonos to pay for my flight from London to Greece so that I would come back after a one-night whirlwind romance where we stayed up all night drinking, pash rashing and talking before I flew out the next morning.

That's a bit full-on and very modern-day romantic but still I found something so endearing about it.

I'm a sucker for that Lana Del Rey–themed romance. I used to make one guy act out her film clips with me. I am such a freakin' weirdo.

With so many great men playing a part in my life, I often wonder why I then looked for the bad in relationships and could never take them further. It wasn't because I thought I was better than the men or that they weren't good enough for me. It wasn't because I wasn't attracted to them. I wasn't afraid of them personally.

Most of the men in my life have treated me with the upmost respect and if anything they treated me like a queen. I have never been overly cheated on either.

It was just a feeling I had. The timing was never right and I guess I was scared. Scared of where this love could take me.

What if I lost myself and became one of those women who gave up all her ambitions for a man and then it all turned to shit and she was left to pick up these sad-sack pieces?

Plus, I believe when you know you just know. When you know then all these fears and make-believe stories will just disappear.

When I know, I won't be scared that something bad will happen because my love will be stronger than my fear. My brain will stop controlling all my senses and my gut and heart will start making the decisions.

That day is coming. I can feel it in my little loins and I am excited.

I want to feel all those feels from all those beautiful men who have crossed my path, in one person. I will have all that in the one partner and I won't ever have to be afraid.

And if it does all shoot to shit I will be okay because I love myself enough now and know myself enough to know that I have got this.

I will be so happy that I have experienced a love so deep and pure and I will be ready and open to keep loving.

Because that, my friends, is life.

Tap out of your head and into your heart, and always remember to take one day at a time, my sunflowers!

ACKNOWLEDGEMENTS

I would like to acknowledge all the good people of the planet. Just to list a few who I have referred to in this book: Nanny Fae, Nanna Kent, Poppy Kent and Pa Jim.

Plus all my beautiful friends who continue to inspire me. Paws and Recover. Oprah Winfrey and Deepak Chopra for getting me through so many dark days simply through an app. Louise Hay and all her work. Gabby Bernstein. My sunflower queen Marie Louise.

Most of all, my mum!

:camera: @angiekent_
:bird: @AngieMKent
:f: @angiekentofficial

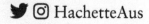 hachette
AUSTRALIA

If you would like to find out more about
Hachette Australia, our authors,
upcoming events and new releases you can
visit our website or our social media channels:

hachette.com.au
 HachetteAustralia
 HachetteAus